The Way of Padre Pio
In His Own Words

Sanctify yourself, and

sanctify others.

M. L. Moncayo

ISBN 979-8-88751-107-8 (paperback)
ISBN 979-8-88751-108-5 (digital)

Christian Faith Publishing
832 Park Avenue
Meadville, PA 16335
www.christianfaithpublishing.com

All Bible quotes are from the New American Bible Revised Edition unless otherwise stated.

Printed in the United States of America

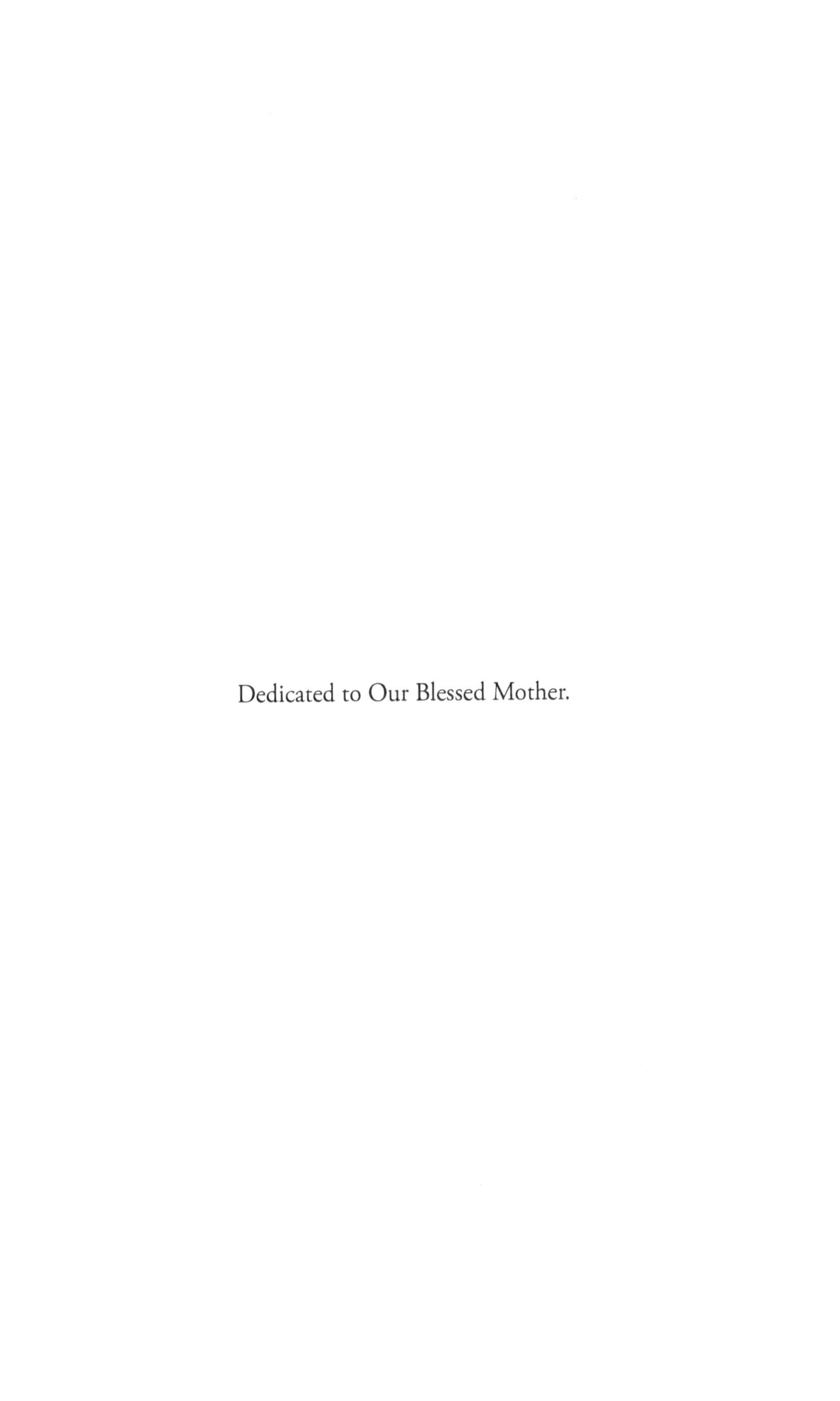

Dedicated to Our Blessed Mother.

Contents

Preface

The great saints of the Catholic faith lived by spiritual principles they believed God had called them to. Those who follow the saints often attempt to live by those same principles, so as to achieve a semblance of that spirituality.

The Way of Padre Pio is an attempt to present the spiritual principles he lived by—the principles of prayer, penance, redemptive suffering and sacrifice, in real-life circumstances, and apply them to our lives.

Most books about St. Padre Pio describe his stigmata, spiritual gifts, and miraculous intercessions. Although *The Way of Padre Pio* includes these, it is more. We may not live his spiritual gifts, but we can live his spiritual principles. His spirituality of redemption was one of love and sacrifice, reparation, and penance. It is the acceptance of what God allows in our life and offering it back to Him for His good purpose, for love of Jesus, for the conversion of sinners, and in reparation for the sins committed against the Immaculate Heart of Mary. We become a living sacrifice of love. So great will be our power of intercession for those we love. Our only limitations for intercessory prayer will be our limit to love and willingness to suffer.

In his own words and life's circumstances, Padre Pio will show us how to walk and live "the way of Padre Pio."

This work is not for the halls of academia, but for the homes of lay people. This is a work to be read in the kitchens where mothers cook and children do their homework. In this work, you will not find deep, theological terms, but words of application. It is all things Catholic—all things Padre Pio.

The Way of Padre Pio will help us to live life following the spiritual principles of Padre Pio, which is to live Christ with love and sacrifice through reparation and penance. In this, we will fulfill what is lacking in the afflictions of Christ on behalf of His body, the church.

Redemptive Suffering Tenets
Living the Redemptive Life through Penance and Reparation

Now I rejoice in my sufferings for your sake, and in my flesh, I am filling up what is lacking in the afflictions of Christ on behalf of his body, which is the church. (Colossians 1:24)

O God, show Yourself more and more to this poor heart of mine, and complete in me the work You have begun. I hear deep within me, a voice which says to me repeatedly—sanctify yourself and sanctify others.[1] (Padre Pio)

There is but one way to save a soul: suffering, united to My suffering on the Cross.[2] (Jesus to St. Faustina)

Join your little sufferings to My Sorrowful Passion, so that they may have infinite value before My Majesty.[3] (Jesus to St. Faustina)

I need your sufferings to rescue souls.[4] (Jesus to St. Faustina)

Pray, pray very much; and make sacrifice for sinners. Many souls are lost, because there are none to make sacrifices for them.[5] (Virgin Mary to Children at Fatima)

Chosen souls are, in My Hand, lights which I cast into the darkness of the world and with which I illumine [sic] it. As stars illumine [sic] the night, so chosen souls illumine [sic] the earth. And the more perfect a soul is, the stronger and the more far-reaching is the light shed by it. It can be hidden and unknown, even to those closest to it, and yet its holiness is reflected in souls even to the most distant extremities of the world.[6] (Jesus to St. Faustina)

---

[1] Allen, 2012, p. 352.
[2] Kowalska, p. 147 (#324).
[3] Ibid, p. 541 (#1512).
[4] Ibid, p. 573 (#1617).
[5] McGlynn, p. 204.
[6] Kowalska, p. 568 (#1601).

Time Well Spent (Preparing for the Way of Padre Pio)

Rising very early before dawn, he left and went
off to a deserted place, where he prayed.

—Mark 1:35

When I want to know more about something, I look for those who know more. If I want to be better at a thing, I seek those who are better than myself. It is the same for spiritual things. I am constantly seeking those have lived or are living the deep spiritual life God is calling me to. Such people I call *Spiritual Giants*. They are the people who have overcome hardships in life and remain obedient to God. There is a saying among Protestants: "It is doubtful whether God can bless a man greatly, until he has hurt him deeply."[1] Those who have been hurt deeply are the people whom God has tried through the difficulties of life. They are both purified and faithful. This allows God to use the person in the most difficult situations knowing they will not be overcome by them, having overcome them already. They have been made to live the deep spiritual life through their trials and remain obedient.

Scripture is filled with such people whose lives God allowed to be crushed by life's circumstances, so He could work in them. The Old Testament has King David who spent time in the desert while being sought after by Saul; Joseph, turned Pharaoh, spent years in prison waiting for God's deliverance after his brothers sold him into slavery; Abraham waited twenty-five years for God to deliver on His promise to give him a son. And there is Job, the ultimate broken man, who lost his family and wealth on the same day, and later his health. His wife could only say, "Curse God and die" (Job 2:9).

The New Testament has its Giants. The Apostle Paul, before God could use him greatly, had to hurt him deeply. Through a series of interventions, Saul learned who the Christian God truly was and received the new name of Paul to signify the new man. His name change was the beginning of a new life. Our Lord constantly challenged Paul through trial and tribulation. He had much to atone for and spent the rest of his life doing so. The will of Saul had to be broken so the will of God could triumph.

* * * * *

In our time, we have great redemptive saints such as St. Faustina Kowalska, St. Mother Teresa of Calcutta, and, of course, St. Padre Pio of Pietrelcina. Each saint learned to surrender themselves, to offer their suffering for the salvation of others, and to say as Paul: "Yet I live, no longer I, but Christ lives in me; insofar as I now live in the flesh, I live by faith in the Son of God who has loved me and given himself up for me" (Galatians 2:20).

The mission and purpose of St. Faustina was to prepare the world for Christ's second coming. Through her, Jesus gave the world her diary, the Divine Mercy image, and Divine Mercy Chaplet. St. Faustina wrote in her diary, "You will prepare the world for My final coming"[2] (Jesus to St. Faustina).

The life of St. Mother Teresa was one of extreme sacrifice and suffering as God called her to the slums of India to be His light in their darkness. In her love and devotion to her Lord and Savior, she wanted to give something beautiful to God, and "drink the Chalice to the last drop."[3]

In a letter to Padre Agostino, Padre Pio described the purpose and mission of his life, "I make good and complete what is still lacking in the Passion of Christ."[4]

The early lives of these saints were spent in preparation for the ministries God would lead them into. For St. Pio, his early years

4

were spent suffering physically through headaches, fevers, constant vomiting, and demonic attacks. These were the "breaking" of a man who God would greatly use until there would be no more Francesco Forgione, only Padre Pio.

How did these Giants survive the suffering of life? What kept their faith from dissolving into nothingness? Or worse, hatred toward God? Were they any different from us in character? Did the times they live in tear at them as ours tears at us? Did they have fewer distractions? Responsibilities? Surely, they were better at knowing God than us!

The difference is this: they learned to say *yes* to God. They *chose* to believe in him, despite what they felt or what they saw. Their time was spent *listening, learning to obey, accepting the pillar* to which they were tied, and ultimately, opening their arms to the cross God had given them and laying down on it. With each cross they bore, every pillar they were tied to, their commitment to follow Him and offer themselves as living sacrifices, to be victims for others, and unite their pain to His on the cross, there came the saving of souls.

By saying yes to Him in the early difficulties of life, they allowed Him to hurt them deeply, to learn obedience as His Son did, that He might use them greatly in the Battle.

How do we learn to say *yes* to the difficulties in our lives? How do we allow Him to hurt us deeply? To do so, we must learn to spend time with the Spiritual Giants, those who learned to say *yes*. Time well spent is time spent with these Spiritual Giants.

* * * * *

How do you spend your time? Will you be ready when the Lord begins the breaking in your life? Is your foundation built to withstand the scourging in life, the burden of the cross He chooses for you? The world has many delights, temptations, and distractions that hold your mind, body, and soul. Will they be enough to sustain you in the battle? Our Lord said, "I have told you this so that you might have peace in me. In the world you will have trouble, but take courage, I have conquered the world" (John 16:33). *Through Him,* you can say the same, but you must live your life *with Him.* You must be crucified to the world *in Him*. What fool enters the darkness without a light? Or rejects the wisdom of those who have traveled the journey you wish to make? You must seek out and spend time with the spiritual giants that have met God in their pain, who learned to say *yes* and submitted themselves to Him. How did they spend time with God? How did they serve Him? What prayers did they pray? What books did they read? How did they learn to hear His voice apart from the world? How did they learn to say *yes* to God in the midst of their suffering?

We have one Giant given to help along the way, Padre Pio. Let us spend time with him who has already walked our path. Listen to his wisdom. Let him speak to our need and show us his way—"the way of Padre Pio."

* * * * *

In His Own Words

On prayer:

> Prayer is the best weapon we have. It is the key to God's Heart. You must speak to Jesus not only with your lips, but with your heart; in fact, on certain occasions, you should speak to Him only with your heart.[5]

> Prayer is the effusion of our heart into God's…when it is well done, it moves the Divine Heart and makes Him always more inclined to grant our requests. Let us pour out our whole soul to God in prayer. He is captivated by our prayers and comes to our aid.[6]

> Pray, hope and don't worry. Worry [sic] is useless. God is merciful and will hear your prayer.[7]

When you find yourself close to God in prayer, speak to Him if you can, and if you are unable to do so stay this way. Let yourself be seen, and do not disturb yourself further.[8]

Souls are saved through continuous prayer.[9]

Prayer must insistent since insistence denotes faith.[10]

You cannot win the battle without prayer.[11]

Never fail to meditate…otherwise you can be sure that you will be beaten later on in everything.[12]

On Scripture:

Meditate on it with attention, examine its elements and search for the hidden meaning. It will then appear to you in all its splendor; it will acquire the power of doing away with your natural materialistic inclinations; it will have the virtue of transforming them into pure and sublime ascensions of the spirit, which will bring together ever more closely your heart with the Divine heart of your Lord.[13]

On life:

We must give an exact account of every moment, of every grace, of every opportunity to do good. The slightest transgression of God's holy laws, will be taken into consideration.[14]

Life is nothing but a continual struggle against oneself, and it does not open to beauty without the price of suffering. Always keep Jesus company in Gethsemane and He will know how to comfort you in the hours of anguish that will come.[15]

Learn to better recognize and adore the divine will in all the events of life.[16]

On suffering:

We do not want to accept the fact that suffering is necessary for our souls, that the Cross must be our daily bread. Just as the body needs nourishment, so does the soul need the Cross day after day, to purify it and detach it from creatures. We do not want to understand that God neither wants nor is able to save or sanctify us without the Cross and the more He draws a soul to Himself, the more he purifies it by means of the Cross.[17]

If you suffer with resignation in doing His will, you do not offend Him, but love Him. And your heart will find great comfort in remembering that in your hour of pain Jesus Himself suffers in you and for you. He did not abandon you when you fled from Him; why should He abandon you now that you are proving your love for Him by the martyrdom of your soul?[18]

By suffering, we have something to give to God. The gift of our pain, of our sufferings, is a great thing, which we cannot do in paradise.[19]

The angels are jealous of us for one reason only: they are not able to suffer for God. Only through suffering can a soul say with certainty, "My God, You see, I do love You!"[20]

Accept all suffering and incomprehension that comes from above. In this way you will perfect and sanctify yourself.[21]

When suffering is endured in a Christian spirit, it will sanctify you… Jesus Himself suffers in you and through you and with you.[22]

If humanity could realize the value of suffering, they would ask for nothing else.[23]

You should humble yourself before God instead of becoming dejected if He reserves for you the sufferings of His Son and wants you to feel your weakness.[24]

On the Mass:

Each holy Mass heard with devotion, produces marvelous effects in our souls, spiritual and material graces, that we ourselves do not know.[25]

It would be easier for the earth to exist without the sun than without the holy sacrifice of the Mass.[26]

On faith:

The most beautiful credo is the one that burst forth from your lips in the dark, as a sacrifice, as a suffering, and with extreme effort to do right.[27]

In the hour of trial, don't tire yourself in trying to find God. He is within you even then, in a most intimate manner. He is with you in your groanings and searching, just like a mother who urges her little child to seek her while she is behind him, and it is precisely her hands that encourage them to reach her.[28]

You are suffering all the effects of divine abandonment, but you have never been abandoned. And it is so, also for other souls who love Jesus. They suffer everything, even the trial of abandonment, but God is always with them. Therefore, be assured that Jesus is always with you and loves you because He is pleased with you. So, don't be afraid; let Jesus treat you as he pleases.[29]

In all human affairs…learn most of all to recognize and adore God's will in everything. Frequently repeat the divine words of our dear Master, 'Thy will be done on earth as it is in heaven.' May this beautiful exclamation always be in your heart and on your lips in all the changes of life. Repeat it in affliction. Repeat it in temptation and in the trials to which Jesus will be pleased to subject you. Repeat it still when you find yourself immersed in the ocean of Jesus' love. This will be your anchor and your salvation.[30]

On Satan:

The field of battle between God and Satan is the human soul. This is where it takes place every moment of our lives. The soul must give free access to our Lord and be completely fortified by Him with every kind of weapon. To put on Jesus Christ, we must die to ourselves.[31]

The devil has but one door through which to enter into our soul; the will. There is no sin, if it has not been committed willfully.[32]

The devil is like a raging dog on a chain; outside the limit of the chain he can bite no one.[33]

Your temptations come from the devil, but your suffering and afflictions come from God… Despise the temptations and embrace the tribulation.[34]

I know the Lord permits the devil to make these assaults. Because His mercy renders you dear to Him, and he wants you to be similar to Him in the anguish of the desert, the Garden and on the Cross.[35]

The Spirit of God is a spirit of peace… The spirit of the devil, instead, excites, exasperates and makes us feel, in that very sorrow, anger against ourselves… Therefore, if any thought agitates you, this agitation never comes from God, who gives you peace, being the Spirit of Peace, but from the devil.[36]

On Mary:

Mother of priests, mediatrix and administratrix of all graces.[37]

Do not be so completely dedicated to Martha's activity that you forget the silence or self-abandonment of Mary.[38]

Always stay close to this heavenly Mother, because she is the sea to be crossed to reach the shores of eternal splendor in the kingdom of dawn.[39]

Some people are so foolish that they think they can go through life without the help of the Blessed Mother.[40]

The shortcut...is the Virgin. The Holy Virgin is the perfect example of God's mercy on earth. She acts as His double. She is the one who brings us a ray of God's immensity and of divine powers.[41]

On the Rosary:

This is my weapon. With this, one wins the battles.[42]

(It is) the synthesis of our faith, the expression of our charity, and the foundation of our hope.[43]

Always recite her Rosary. That is the armor against the evils of the world today.[44]

Satan wants to destroy this prayer, but in this he will never succeed. The Rosary is the prayer of those who triumph over everything and everyone. It was our Lady who taught us this prayer, just as it was Jesus who taught us the Our Father.[45]

On prayer, suffering, and reparation:

> You think you know my love for you, but you don't know it is much greater than you can imagine. I follow you with my prayers, with my suffering, and with my tears.[46]

> Then we shall be offering the most beautiful, the most noble of prayers because our prayers will have sprung from sacrifice.[47]

> It is true that God's power triumphs over everything, but humble and suffering prayer prevails over God Himself.[48]

> Physical and spiritual ills are the most worthy offering you can make to Him who saved you by suffering.[49]

On heaven:

> Every sacrifice we make on earth will be recompensed. Heaven is total joy, continuous joy. We will be constantly thanking God. It's useless to try to figure out exactly what heaven is like, because we can't understand it, but when the veil of this life is taken off, we will understand things in a different way. No suffering, no matter how low the motive on which it rests will go unrewarded in eternal life.[50]

> Your child is in paradise, watching over you, assisting you, smiling on you, and preparing a place for you.[51] (To a couple who lost their child)

* * * * *

What fool enters the darkness without a light or rejects the wisdom of those who have traveled the journey you wish to make? Spend time with those who have walked the spiritual path. Listen to their wisdom. Let them speak to your needs. Let them help you walk "the way of Padre Pio."

Additional Quotes on Suffering

My son, you would have abandoned Me if I hadn't crucified you. Under the Cross, one learns to love.[52]

Love Jesus, love Him a lot, but to do this, be ready to love sacrifice more.[53]

The good-hearted man is always strong; he suffers, he sheds tears and he consoles himself sacrificing himself for God and his neighbor.[54]

He who begins to love, must be ready to suffer.[55]

If I know a person is afflicted, whether in body or in soul, what I would not do for the Lord to see that person freed from his ailments? For his salvation I would willingly take on all his afflictions, if the Lord permitted, I would give up the fruits of these sufferings for him.[56]

Jesus keeps repeating, "Do not fear, I will make you suffer, but I will also give you strength. I wish your soul to be tried and purified through this daily and hidden martyrdom. Do not be frightened if I permit the demon to torture you, the world to displease you, the people you hold most dear to afflict you, because nothing can prevail against those who, for love of Me, groan under the weight of the cross."[57]

Jesus tells me that in moments of love, it is He who pleases me, and it is I who in moments of sorrow, please Him… Likewise, the comfort one can give to Jesus not only in bearing His sorrows with Him and when He finds a soul, who, for love of Him, asks not for consolations but to participate in His very sorrows is incomprehensible… But when He wants to be delighted, He speaks to me of His sorrows, He invites me—with a voice full of both supplication and authority—to affix my body (to the cross) in order to alleviate His suffering.[58]

---

[1] Tozer, p. 165.
[2] Kowalska, p. 190 (#429).
[3] Teresa, p. 29.
[4] Ruffin, p. 75.
[5] Pio, 2018, p. 24.
[6] Ibid, p. 23.
[7] Ibid, p. 24.
[8] Ibid, p. 27.
[9] Ibid, p. 28.
[10] Ibid, p. 28.
[11] Ibid, p. 36.
[12] Ibid, p. 37.
[13] Ibid, p. 31.
[14] Ibid, p. 7.
[15] Ibid, pp. 175–176.
[16] Ibid, p. 15.
[17] Ibid, p. 44.
[18] Ibid, p. 52.
[19] Ibid, p. 49.
[20] Ibid, p. 57.
[21] Ibid, p. 58.
[22] Ibid, p. 193.
[23] Allen, 2012, p. 5.

24 Pio, 2018, p. 156.
25 Ibid, p. 119.
26 Ibid, p. 119.
27 Ibid, p. 128.
28 Pio, 1999, p. 104.
29 Ibid, p. 133.
30 Ruffin, p. 174.
31 Pio, 2018, p. 99.
32 Ibid, p. 74.
33 Ibid, p. 74.
34 Ibid, p. 64.
35 Ibid, p. 62–63.
36 Ibid, pp. 199–200.
37 Ibid, p. 86.
38 Ibid, p. 87.
39 Ibid, p. 88.
40 Allen, 2012, p. 34.
41 Ruffin, p. 177.
42 Napolitano, p. 217.
43 Allen, 2012, p. 33.
44 Ibid, p. 50.
45 Ibid, p. 34.
46 Allen, 2011, p. 233.
47 Ibid, p. 67.
48 Ruffin, p. 174.
49 Ibid, p. 176.
50 Ibid, p. 176.
51 Ibid, p. 176.
52 Epistolario I, p. 339.
53 Pio, 2018, p. 50.
54 Ibid, p. 50.
55 Ibid, p. 51.
56 Pio, 2003, p. 66.
57 Ibid, p. 47.
58 Ibid, p. 44.

The Wrong End of Suffering
(Sanctify Yourself)

He who begins to love, must be ready to suffer.[1]

—Padre Pio

When we think of sacrifice, we think of suffering. When we are offered opportunities to sacrifice for others, and therefore, suffer, we say, "Oh, that is more than I am able to do. The cost is too high. I am too busy." In our humanity, this is normal. This is what our Lord struggled with in His humanity in the garden. "He advanced a little and fell prostrate in prayer, saying, 'My Father, if it is possible, let this cup pass from me; yet, not as I will, but as you will'" (Matthew 26:39).

In our sacrifice, we look at the wrong end of suffering. Let me tell you a story shared by a close friend.

He got a call from the babysitter of his grandchildren. Her voice was nervous. She began, "I am sorry to have to tell you, but you are his dad, and you wanted to know."

Earlier that day, his son, the sitter, and grandkids were walking in a department store when it happened. His son fell onto the floor. When the security guard tried to help him up, the son pushed him away. It was then the guard smelled the liquor on the son. The helping guard became the security guard he was paid to be and tossed the son out of the store. The grandkids were horrified. But they saw this a lot at home. That call broke the heart of a parent. The son is an alcoholic. His alcoholism would be the cause the children would be taken from him.

At that moment, my friend cried to the Lord to let him take the pain of his son, to allow my friend to carry and bear it, so his son could find healing. What parent would not run into a burning building to save their child from the flames or stand between them and an oncoming car to protect their child? In that moment, no parent is saying, "The cost is too high. That is more than I am able to do."

We focus on the wrong end of suffering.

When the sitter called, my friend did not see the high cost of sacrifice. In fact, he sought the opposite. He begged the Lord for his son's pain, to put it on him, and allow my friend to make the reparation needed to allow God's grace into his son's life. He would pay any cost!

My friend asked God what He would accept as reparation. In his prayer time, he remembered the loneliness of our Lord in the garden, saying to the disciples, "Could you not wait one hour with Me?" What my friend heard was "Peter. John. I hurt. I struggle. I am lonely. Stay with Me. I need your companionship." The answer to his question came. "Spend time with Me. I need your companionship."

Three hours before the Blessed Sacrament from 12:00 a.m. to 3:00 a.m. each Friday during Lent is what my friend offered. He would keep Jesus company. He struggled and did not always stay awake, but he was there. As he was telling the story, his eyes teared up and said his son had been with him, in spirit, as were all those he brought with him to the garden to be with Jesus.

* * * * *

The secret to sacrifice is love and motivation. We do because we love. We love; therefore, we do. And we sacrifice for those we love. Our Lord said to Saint Faustina, "There is but one price a soul is bought: suffering united to My suffering on the Cross."[2]

But we focus on the wrong end of sacrifice.

> I suffer not for suffering's sake, but for the fruits it brings.[3] (Padre Pio)

St. Pio knew early in his life what his vocation would be. He wrote to his superior, Father Benedetto:

> For a long time, I have felt in myself a need to offer myself to the Lord as a victim for poor sinners and for the souls in Purgatory. This desire has been growing continually in my heart so that it has now become what I would call a strong passion…, imploring on Him to lay on me the punishments prepared for sinners and for souls in Purgatory so long as He converts and saves sinners and quickly releases the souls in Purgatory. It seems to me that Jesus wants this.[4]

Soon after this realization, Francesco Forgione received both the stigmata and transverberation—wounds belonging to the Passion of Christ—that would lead to the full participation of Padre Pio in the Mass with Jesus. It was through this participation of both wounds and Passion in the Mass, "as a victim for poor sinners and for the souls in Purgatory", the mission of reparation and expiation of sins would come.

Padre Pio looked at the right end of suffering, "the fruits it brings."

* * * * *

When our Lord said, "No one has greater love than this, to lay down one's life for one's friends," (John 15:13), He stated His own sacrificial love for us. His suffering, freely given, expiates the sin in our lives. As we offer our sacrifice on the behalf of another, *united to the sacrifice and suffering of our Lord*, we offer reparation or amends for their sins, allowing God to work in the person's life without the hindrance of their sin. Suffering becomes the currency of redemption and healing. It covers the debt of another by offering suffering to pay the debt. Suffering is the only offering accepted by the Father to remove sin. It must be freely given, empowered by His love. Sacrifice alone is insufficient. It is a finite act done in finite time. When the act of sacrifice is empowered by His eternal love, it has eternal value. This is needed because He is eternal. The sacrifice is accepted by the Father because it is done through His love.

Jesus, speaking to St. Catherine of Siena, had much to say on this.

> I, who am Infinite, seek infinite works, that is an infinite perfection of love. I wish therefore that the works of penance, and of other corporal exercises, should be observed merely as a means, not as the fundamental affection of the soul. For, if the principal affection of the soul were placed in penance, I should receive a finite thing like a word, which when it has issued from the mouth, is no more, unless it have issued with affection of the soul, which conceives and brings forth virtue in truth; that is, unless the finite operation, which I have called a word, should be joined with the affection of love, in which case it would be grateful and pleasant to Me.[5]

The affection of love Jesus speaks of is the focus of who we are in Him. It is His love in us. In this, we give back what is given from Him.

> It is true, however, that that act, unless made through love of Me, profits him nothing so far as grace is concerned…for in the love of Me is fulfilled and completed the love of thy neighbor, and the Law observed. For he, only, can be of use in his state of life, who is bound to Me with this love.[6]

This love is accepted by Him because it comes from Him. It is His love. It motivates us to sacrifice for others and to be used as a sacrifice. The Infinite Love (Holy Spirit) that moves us to sacrifice gives the act *infinite value* because it comes from Him and is therefore accepted by Him. The degree to which we are willing to sacrifice only measures the degree of love that empowers it. The purer the love, the greater the ability to suffer. This sacrificial love we know is the Passion of Christ. As He sacrifices out of love for us, so we sacrifice out of love for Him *and our neighbor.* In this, we fulfill what is lacking in His afflictions. What is lacking is His love sacrificing for others—through us. In this, we become like Him. "Suffering is a great grace; through suffering the soul becomes like the Savior; in suffering the soul becomes crystalized"[7] (Jesus to St. Faustina). Jesus is saying, "As I sacrificed Myself for you, so you must sacrifice for others through Me, and complete the work of salvation I began. In this, you sanctify yourself and others." And St. Pio had much of it to give.

In His agony in the garden, Jesus focused not on the suffering, but on His love for us, and the healing it would bring. That healing end is called the Passion of the Christ.

* * * * *

When God is allowing pain in your life, unite your pain to the sacrifice of the Mass. Place your pain in the offertory for someone you are praying for. This act sanctifies both you and the one prayed for.

We may not have the stigmata or transverberation as Padre Pio. We may not wear the crown of thorns or have our backs scourged, but we carry wounds on our bodies and bruises in our souls. There is pain enough. For those who love, there is more. We will suffer because we love because Christ loves in us. So when suffering comes, look at the right end, the end with healing. For St. Pio, suffering was his daily bread.

* * * * *

Healing came to my friend's son and continues to come. He is on the road to recovery. His children are back with him. In the consecration of his son and kids to Mother Mary and St. Pio, healing is coming to them all.

In His Own Words

Rising above selfishness, we must bow down to the sufferings and wounds of our fellow men. We must make them our own, knowing how to suffer with our brethren for the love of God. We must know how to instill hope into their hearts and bring back a smile to their lips, having restored a ray of light into their souls. Then we shall be offering God the most beautiful, the most noble of prayers, because our prayers will have sprung from sacrifice.[8]

I am an entire wound. There is nothing in me which has not been attacked by suffering.[9]

The Kingdom of Heaven is reached by prayer and suffering.[10]

We do not want to accept the fact that suffering is necessary for our souls; that the Cross must be our daily bread. Just as the body needs nourishment, so does the soul need the Cross, day after day, to purify it and detach it from creatures. We do not want to understand that God neither wants nor is able to save or sanctify us without the Cross and the more he draws a soul to Himself, the more He purifies it by means of the Cross.[11]

Everyone on this earth has a cross; therefore, we must be careful not to be like the bad thief, but rather like the good one.[12]

Your state is not one of punishment, but one of exquisite love. Therefore, bless the Lord for this, and resign yourself to drinking the chalice of Gethsemane.[13]

By suffering we have something to give to God. The gift of our pain, of our sufferings is a great thing, which we cannot do in Paradise.[14]

The angels are jealous of us for one reason only: they are not able to suffer for God. Only through suffering can a soul say with certainty, "My God, You see I do love You!"[15]

I offer myself as a victim for everyone.[16]

If humanity could realize the value of suffering, they would ask for nothing else.[17]

---

[1] Pio, 2018, p. 51.

[2] Michalenko, p. 80 (#324).

[3] da Cervinara, p. 22.

[4] Ruffin, p. 74.

[5] Catherine, p. 21.

[6] Ibid, p. 15.

[7] Michalenko, p. 55 (#57).

[8] Allen, 2011, pp. 66–67.

[9] Galeone, Dom Pierino. "Together With Padre Pio: Booklet One." September 18, 2015. www.lecatechesididonvincenzocarone.wordpress.com. INSIEME CON PADRE PIO—Booklet I°. p. 4

[10] Napolitano, p. 95.

[11] Pio, 2018, p. 44.

[12] Ibid, p. 44–45.

[13] Ibid, p. 47.

[14] Ibid, p. 49.

[15] Ibid, p. 57.

[16] Ibid, p. 122.

[17] Allen, 2012, p. 5.

Redemptive Suffering

There is but one price at which souls are bought, and that
is suffering united to My suffering on the Cross.[1]

—Jesus to Saint Faustina

Before the existence of time, space, or intelligence, it was decided
by the Infinite a creature would be made in Its image with all Its
attributes. The purpose of this creation was to love and worship its
Creator. Knowing one attribute would be its downfall—free will,
and choose to disobey—the Infinite through another attribute—
love, would take the form of Its creation called man to restore what
was lost. In the love of the Infinite for Its creation was the willingness
to heal the broken relationship by taking the form of Its creation.
This would cost the human life of the One chosen to restore what
was lost.

God, the Father, from the beginning, has deemed that suffering—offered freely in love to pay another's debt—will expiate the
debt of sin. This human debt of disobedience has been paid for by
the human death of the Second Person of the Infinite, Jesus Christ.
It is the standard by which all debt of disobedience is paid. This
standard is given to us to find forgiveness in Him and to offer our
own pain and suffering, united to His on the Cross, to bring healing
to others.

It is in this standard our life's suffering can find purpose and
healing. This makes suffering redeemable. In His Hands, all suffering
is redemptive.

There is ability to redeem in everything we do, in every aspect of life. *Redemption* lies within our listening and in our speaking, while we eat and while we sleep, in our love and in our hate. Every act has the potential of redemption. Redemption can be found when what we are doing is offered to God for His good purpose, to use as He desires. Every act can be purified, sanctified, and multiplied unto His good pleasure. Redemption is creating eternal value from a finite action.

When we learn to embrace the pain in our life and offer it for others, it has purpose. When our joy and good works are given to His good pleasure, grace abounds even more.

* * * * *

In Victor Frankl's book, *Man's Search for Meaning*, he describes his life as a Jewish doctor in the German World War II concentration camps. The constant suffering of each prisoner was more than unbearable—it was unlivable. Dr. Frankl describes daily life in an event while at the infirmary.

> I spent some time in a hut for typhus patients who ran very high temperatures and were often delirious, many of them moribund. After one of them had just died, I watched without any emotional upset the scene that followed, which was repeated over and over again with each death. One by one the prisoners approached the still warm body. One grabbed the remains of a messy meal of potatoes; another decided that the corpse's wooden shoes were an improvement on his own, and exchanged them. A third man did the same with the dead man's coat... All this I watched with unconcern. Eventually, I asked the "nurse" to remove the body... The man with the corpse approached the steps. Wearily he dragged himself up. Then the body: first the feet, then

the trunk, and finally—with uncanny rattling noise—the head of the corpse bumped up the two steps.[2]

He continues,

> My place was on the opposite side of the hut, next to the small, sole window, which was built near the floor. While my cold hands clasped a bowl of hot soup from which I sipped greedily, I happened to look out the window. The corpse which had just been removed stared in at me with glazed eyes. Two hours before I had spoken to that man. Now I continued sipping my soup.[3]

Living in conditions that appeared would never change, the "living" had become dead inside to all. Apathy had grown in the place where love and concern had lived. According to Dr. Frankl, later a renowned psychotherapist, this was a natural progression for circumstances that appear to have no hope of changing. For the prisoners alive in the camps, it was an emotional death.

Dr. Frankl, surviving the camps, went on to write,

> Every day, every hour, offered the opportunity to make a decision, a decision which determined whether you would or would not submit to those powers which threatened to rob you of your very self, your inner freedom; which determined whether or not you would become the plaything of circumstance, renouncing freedom and dignity to become molded into the form of the typical inmate.[4]

He speaks of those prisoners who choose not to allow circumstance to dictate who they were, or would become. These men showed compassion and relief to others while suffering themselves. It was Victor Frankl's answer to man's search for meaning:

> A man who becomes conscious of the responsibility he bears toward a human being who affectionately waits for him…will never be able to throw away his life. He knows the "why" for his existence, and will be able to bear almost any "how."[5]

Those who survived the camps had lived with meaning and purpose, giving them the strength to survive their suffering. Whether the purpose and meaning lay in the value of their own life, or in another's, it gave reason to live. Every action moved a prisoner toward life or death. Without purpose, the path was toward death.

In our Christian life, we have our "why" for existence: we are created out of love *to love* our Creator. Now, we must choose the "how." God has shown the way to love Him. *There is no greater love than to lay down one's life for another.* This purpose will keep us from the apathy of life, from an emotional death and living dead to others. How do we lay down our lives daily for others? We offer our pain and suffering, united to the Cross, as debt for their offences against God. Our pain is their healing.

In offering our pain to Christ and for others, we fulfill the two greatest commandments: love your God with all your heart, and love your neighbor as yourself. If our "why" in life is to love God with all our heart, then our "how" lies in loving our neighbor. In doing so, we live the Passion of Christ. Again, this is "the way of Padre Pio." We were created to love God; we express this by loving God and others, specifically by laying down our lives for them.

Redemptive Suffering

Redemptive Suffering is the use of one's suffering as compensation for another's sin. In Christian theology, it is the offer of Christ's suffering and death as full payment for the justice demanded of God against sin. For Christians, it is the offer for God to place the consequences of another's sin onto oneself, to make amends for that person, and allow God to work graces into the life of the other without the hindrance of their sin. It is the offering of our suffering and sacrifice, freely given, *united to the Sacrifice of the Cross*, that redeems sin and makes reparation for it. The value of the reparation lies not in the suffering, but in the love that offers it; the value of the love lies in the intensity that tests the strength of that love. The greater the sacrifice, the purer the love. It is this sacrifice that proves our love for Him which then opens our soul to His will and Spirit. Each suffering leads us away from ourselves and closer to Him. In this sacrifice for another, we become intercessors.

Offering reparation for others may include the willingness to take onto oneself the actual illness or circumstances of the person such as Padre Pio did. The reparation can also be a general gesture given to God to use as He wishes such as praying a novena.

No action of our own can expiate sin. Only the sacrifice of the Cross can do this. It is when we unite our sacrifice with the sacrifice of the Cross does it have power. The act itself is meaningless unless it is united to the Cross. It is the Cross that gives it value, the *standard* that lives within the act. The *standard* is the selfless love of God. His love, *through the offering of our suffering and sacrifice*, makes reparation for sin. We cannot take on another's sin; we can only make reparation for the consequences of sin.

Saint Pope John Paul II explains Redemptive Suffering and the saint's role in the salvation of each other:

> Does that mean that the Redemption achieved by Christ is not complete? No. It only means that the Redemption, accomplished through satisfactory love, remains always open to all love expressed in human suffering. In this dimension—the dimension of love—the Redemption which has already been completely accomplished is, in a certain sense, constantly being accomplished. Christ achieved the

Redemption completely and to the very limits, but at the same time He did not bring it to a close. In this Redemptive Suffering, through which the Redemption of the world was accomplished, Christ opened Himself from the beginning to every human suffering and constantly does so. Yes, it seems to be part of the very essence of Christ's Redemptive Suffering that this suffering requires to be unceasingly complete.[6] (Apostolic Letter Salvifici Doloris of the Supreme Pontiff John Paul II to the bishops, to the priests, to the religious families and to the Faithful of the Catholic Church on the Christian meaning of human suffering, February 11, 1984)

Forms of Redemptive Suffering

Redemptive suffering has many forms. The simplest form is *surrendering our will to God*. The *Morning Offering Prayer* guides us through this daily task.

O Jesus, through the Immaculate Heart of Mary, I offer you my prayers, works, joys, and sufferings of this day for all the intentions of Your Sacred Heart, in union with the Holy Sacrifice of the Mass throughout the world, for the salvation of souls, the reparation of sins, the reunion of all Christians, and in particular for the intentions of the Holy Father this month. Amen.[7]

In this prayer, we commit to God every act performed through the day to God to use in the manner He knows best. In this way, *everything* we do becomes holy. We become immersed in His life to the point where everything we do, we examine, so we can offer it to God. St. Pio reminds us, "We must give an exact account of every moment, of every grace, of every holy inspiration, of every opportunity to do good."[8] St. Mother Teresa taught us that every missed prayer, every missed act of kindness is one less drop of mercy in the sea of God's love for all eternity.

A second form is the act of *self-examination*. We must be free of sin. As we present ourselves to God, we ask Him to illuminate our conscience. We cannot change what we do not know is wrong. By His grace, we offer the only thing that is ours, our will and intellect. In that is the beginning of self-knowledge and the removal of all that is not of God from our lives. In the removal of such, great is our power to intercede. "I demand of you a perfect and whole-burnt offering; an offering of the will. No other sacrifice can compare with this one"[9] (Jesus to St. Faustina).

As God shows us our wrongs and weaknesses through self-examination, we approach Him through confession. In confession, we are given prayers and acts by the priest to show repentance. We may be asked to perform an act to correct the sinful nature that caused the sin. This may include performing an act of kindness for someone we were impatient with. This allows God's grace into that part of ourselves that allowed the sin to occur whereby we begin to decrease so He may increase.

A third form is *obedience*. Obedience to the Father's will reveals our relationship to Him. Do I obey Him when He asks me to help carry His cross and nails me to it? Do I obey Him when He allows suffering in my life, and I cannot find Him anywhere? Do I obey when it costs me everything? It was through love and obedience Jesus lived His Passion out. Jesus granted St. Faustina a request through her obedience to her confessor. "I have granted the grace you asked for on behalf of that soul, but not because of the mortification you choose for yourself, but because of the act of complete obedience to My representative did I grant grace to that soul for whom you interceded and begged mercy. Know that when you mortify your own self-will, then Mine reigns within you."[10] Herein lies the crux: in the darkest of times, in the silence of His voice, when obeying costs me everything I love, do I obey my will or His?

A fourth form is *prayer*. Prayer is the door to the Father's heart which, when done in the most difficult times of trial, can turn His heart toward the one praying. It is in the form of novenas, chaplets, and, of course, the beloved Rosary. It is standing in His presence without uttering a word, a simple offering of one's joyful or broken heart. Prayer can be offered as reparation, purification, and in the veneration of saints as we ask for their intercession. A novena said for nine days, a rosary offered on our knees at the feet of the parish Madonna, the Chaplet of Divine Mercy prayed at the three o'clock hour, and skipping a meal to pray are not only forms of prayer but ways to make reparation for others. Our Lady at Fatima urged the children to pray and sacrifice for the conversion of sinners and the offenses against her Immaculate Heart and the Sacred Heart of Jesus. She gave the children a prayer to be said before a sacrifice and reparation were offered:

> O Jesus, it is for Your love, for the conversion of sinners, and in reparation for the sins committed against the Immaculate Heart of Mary.[11]

When we pray for others, we intercede for them. Our prayers become intercessory prayers. The *Mass* is the greatest form of intercession because it is the greatest form of prayer. It is the sacrifice of the Son of God. There is no greater power or entity than the Blood of Jesus covering a soul. It removes sin and its consequences. It empowers a soul with the Spirit of God. "He himself bore our sins in his body upon the cross, so that, free from sin, we might live for righteousness. By his wounds you have been healed" (1 Peter 2:24). Outside the sacrifice of the Mass, our actions are nothing, until they are united with Him. In the Mass, we can intercede for those we pray for by offering them during the Intentions of the Mass. We can say, "Lord, I offer (your petition here) for the intention of the sacrifice of this Mass. Remove from them sin that hinders Your grace. I offer my life as reparation, united to Your sacrifice on the Cross."

We can place them on the altar at the time of the Offertory and say, "Father, I offer You the Body, Blood, Soul, and Divinity of Your dearly beloved Son, our Lord Jesus Christ, in atonement for the sins of ———."

Few are called to be a Victim Soul to the degree St. Pio, St. Faustina, and Mother Teresa were. These souls are so close to Christ they bare His marks in some form. Their mission was to help Jesus bear His cross and live out the motto: "Not my will, but Thy will be done." Nothing happens, but first prayer.

Work of Intercessors

God can work in a person's life without that person asking Him directly for help because *another has interceded* for them, and God honors that. God honors the intercession for another because the act of taking on the consequences of that other's sin *through suffering* was done freely. It is an act of shear love and grace, done in the standard of God's love. The consequences of that person's sin through suffering are put onto the intercessor. This is what Christ did for mankind. Again, it can only be done when the suffering is united to the suffering of Christ on the Cross, the Standard of Redemption.

> My sacrifice is nothing in itself, but, when I
> join it to the sacrifice of Jesus Christ, it becomes
> all-powerful and has the power to appease divine
> wrath.[12] (St. Faustina)

This desire to offer oneself cannot come from within us as "I know that good does not dwell in me" (Romans 7:18). It is His call in us, the Passion of Christ, that moves us. It is His Passion in us that moves us to bear another's physical, emotional, or spiritual blight; it is His Passion that moves us to deny ourselves to save another. This is what is meant in the verse, "No one has greater love than this, to lay down one's life for one's friends" (John 15:13). In offering to take another's consequences of sin through suffering, we redeem the other and pay the debt of that sin. We, then, "complete what is lacking in Christ's afflictions for the sake of his body" (Colossians 1:24). We become Christ for them. The sin that prevents Christ from freely working in a person's life, redemptive suffering removes.

We cannot "save" another person, but we can intercede for them, through our suffering, united to Christ's suffering on the Cross. Through the sacrifice of Christ, sin is atoned, expiated. The Cross of Christ is the only altar the Father will accept as atonement for sin. Through the sacrifice of our suffering, the consequences of sin are amended. The effects of sin are removed from the person we are praying for and placed on us. We pray to God, as Padre Pio prayed, to lay on us the punishments that are prepared for sinners and for souls in purgatory, so long as He converts and saves them.

In the laying down of our lives as intercessors, Christ may show us areas where we are lacking in Him and where He desires a change. Before we can offer ourselves, we must let Him alter and purify us where He wishes and allow us to "come up" to His standard. An offering of self must be clean of all blemishes. This is why self-examination and confession are important. Therefore, attend confession regularly and pray:

> Lord, remove from my life all that is not of
> the Father. I ask this through the intercession of
> Mother Mary, St. Joseph and St. Padre Pio.

In daily living, I ask Him to remove what is not of the Father in what I am doing at the moment. It makes all the difference, especially when what I am doing is frustrating or doubtful.

Redemptive Suffering Saints

Throughout Scripture, there have been saints who offered themselves as reparation for others. These are Redemptive Suffering or Intercessory saints. Moses, when God threatened to obliterate the Hebrews due to their stubbornness, offered himself as atonement for them (Exodus 32:30–34). St. Paul of Tarsus not only offered his sufferings for the Body of Christ but did so gladly (Colossians 1:24). We may not be so bold in our offerings as the saints of old, but as St. Therese of Lisieux, we can offer the little things in our daily lives.

St. Mother Teresa

The life of St. Mother Teresa of Calcutta (1910–1997) was one of Redemptive Suffering. In her call from Jesus, He told her, "Come be My Light. In your immolation of Me, and your love for Me, they will see Me, know Me, want Me."[13]

By embracing their darkness and suffering, she was bringing them to the Light. As she took on the poverty of those she served, she also took on their despair. This "darkness" became her suffering that she offered for their salvation. Offering to make amends for their sins through her sacrifice, God accepted it. Her suffering was the vessel on which her prayer rose to Heaven.

St. Faustina Kowalska

The short life of St. Maria Faustina Kowalska (1905–1938) set the stage for the final coming of our Lord. Through her submission and intercession, Jesus gave the Novena to the Divine Mercy prayer, His picture as the Divine Mercy and the diary of St. Faustina. Jesus told her, "My daughter, I want to instruct you on how you are to rescue souls through sacrifice and prayer. You will save more souls through prayer and sacrifice than will a missionary through his teachings and sermons alone. I want to see you as a sacrifice of living love, which only then carries weight before Me. You must be annihilated, destroyed, living as if you were dead in the most sacred depths of your being… And great will be your power for whomever you intercede."[14] This mission carries through our time, still saving souls through the Divine Mercy.

St. Padre Pio

Padre Pio knew the Lord was calling him to do exactly this—take upon himself the punishments due to those he prayed for so

God could work in their lives. In the beginning, he did not know the extent of the call. Saint Pio wrote about this to his superior:

> For some time I have felt the need to offer myself to the Lord as a victim for poor sinners and for souls in Purgatory… imploring Him to inflict me with the punishments that are prepared for sinners and for souls in Purgatory…so long as he converts and saves sinners.[15]

The life of Padre Pio was one of redemptive suffering. His mission was to be Christ on earth as a Victim Soul. In that life, he was to offer his suffering for mankind through his wounds, illnesses, demonic and personal attacks. For fifty-eight years, he offered himself for his spiritual children, unsaved souls, and world events. As his spiritual children, we are called to do the same in whatever capacity God calls us to. When we offer our suffering for the purification of others, we ourselves are purified. St. Pio will assist us as we do this. Assuring a spiritual child of his help, he said, "Rest assured that I will pray for you. Even after my death, I will remember you in my prayers."[16]

This was the passion of Padre Pio. It was the mission he asked for and received from Jesus when he was given the stigmata. This must be our passion, the Passion of Christ in us.

Life Happens

Suffering is natural. It occurs in life alongside joy and happiness. God is the author of both (Ecclesiastes 7:13–14). In this process, we trust God to allow whatever He chooses to bring into our lives. We do not need to create suffering. Padre Pio tells us which sufferings are best to offer: "Physical and spiritual ills are the most worthy offering you can make to Him who saved you by suffering."[17]

God has His plans for us. We need only seek His guidance through the suffering.

> And I saw that nothing truly happens by accident or luck, but everything by God's wise providence…for matters that have been in God's foreseeing wisdom, since before time began, befall us suddenly, all unawares; and so, in our blindness and ignorance we say that this is an accident of luck, but to our Lord it is not so.[18]
> (St. Julian of Norwich)

As life happens, suffering becomes meaningful because we choose to offer it for another. The focus of our pain moves from us to the one we offer it for. When a suffering is offered, two spiritual graces occur: the suffering is placed into the palm of God where Satan cannot touch it (Isaiah 49:16); the offering allows God to bring His grace to another. The person who offers the sacrifice is sanctified; the person for whom the sacrifice is offered is sanctified. Suffering is used for purification. It is how God sanctifies us. However horrible the suffering is, given to our Lord, it has redemption. "I demand, My daughter, that your sacrifice be pure and full of humility, that I may find pleasure in it. I will not spare My grace, that you may be able to fulfill what I demand of you…accept all sufferings with love… All power rests in the will"[19] (Jesus to St. Faustina).

* * * * *

When we offer our actions to God, at best, we move closer to Him; at worst, we keep Satan from using them against us. Either way, our actions are eternal. They count for and against us. In His hands, "We know all things work together for good to those who are called according to His purpose" (Romans 8:28).

We long to help those we love and care for and gladly participate in the alleviation of their pain by offering up our own to allow God's grace of healing in theirs. Jesus will *not interfere* with the free will of a person, but He will *honor the suffering intercession* of another as the Father honored and accepted the suffering intercession of His Son for all humankind. As we participate in the Passion of Christ and complete His redemptive work, we will be suffering for one another *through* the Passion, *with* the Passion, and *in* the Passion of Christ. It is "the way of Padre Pio."

In His Own Words

You think you know my love for you, but you don't know that it is much greater than you can imagine. I follow you with my prayers, with my suffering, and with my tears.[20]

Oh God, there is so much suffering, so much sickness. Please take away the sufferings of that poor man and give them to me.[21]

If you had even a part of the pain that I have, you would die.[22]

I am ready for anything, as long as Jesus is content to save the souls of my brothers, especially those He has entrusted to my care.[23]

I feel all your troubles as if they were my own.[24]

The angels are jealous of us for one reason only: they are not able to suffer for God. Only through suffering can a soul say with certainty: "My God, You see, I do love You."[25]

The gift of our pain, of our sufferings is a great thing, which we cannot do in Paradise.[26]

1. Michalenko, p. 80 (#324).
2. Frankl, pp. 33–35.
3. Ibid, p.35.
4. Ibid, p. 104.
5. Ibid, p. 127.
6. Pope John Paul II. "Apostolic Letter,"
7. Gautrelet, "Morning Offering Prayer."
8. Pio, 2018, p. 7.
9. Faustina, p. 358 (#923).
10. Ibid, p.164 (#365).
11. McGlynn, p. 204.
12. Michalenko, p. 110 (#482).
13. Teresa, p. 98.
14. Faustina, p. 627 (#1767).
15. Ruffin, p. 74.
16. Allen, 2011, p. 145.
17. Ruffin, p. 176.
18. Pearson, p. 60.
19. Faustina, p. 627 (#1767).
20. Allen, 2011, p. 233.
21. Ibid, p. 62.
22. Ibid, p. 262.
23. Ibid, p. 222.
24. Allen, 2012, p.65.
25. Pio, 2018, p. 57.
26. Pio, 2018, p. 49.

To Live Is Christ and to Die Is Gain (Sanctify Others)

What a nasty thing it is to live by the heart! It means
living at every moment a death that never kills, or
experiencing a living death and a dying life.[1]

—Padre Pio

Walking through an antique store, I caught a glimpse of a wall
plaque. Its saying caught my eye. It is the meaning of redemptive
suffering. It read:

> I asked Jesus, "How much do You love me?"
> "This much," He answered. Then stretched out
> His arms and died.

To pay another's debt so that the other may go free, and do so
every moment of one's life, is the life of the Victim Soul, the embod-
iment of living and dying in Christ. Saint Catherine of Sienna was
such a soul. Jesus said to her,

> Very pleasing to Me, dearest daughter, is
> the willing desire to bear every pain and fatigue,
> even unto death, for the salvation of souls, for the
> more the soul endures, the more she shows that
> she loves Me; loving Me she comes to know more
> of My truth, and the more she knows, the more

pain and intolerable grief she feels at the offenses
committed against Me.[2]

How one bares their pain, its manner and kind, is as different as the person baring it. Jesus continues with St. Catherine, "For
this reason, (if the soul should elect to love Me) she should elect to
endure pains for Me in whatever mode or circumstance I may send
them to her."[3]

Most of us ask God to remove our pain. Few ask to tolerate it.
Even less ask Him to place it upon us. The life of a Victim Soul seeks
to be the holder of pain, the scapegoat for another's debt. It is a life
of sacrifice and denial, the death of one's will and surrender to His.
It is a life given to Him for His good purpose, to lose the bonds of
sin and worldly corruption in a life, to be the victim that will pay the
price for another's sin.

Many came to St. Pio for healing. Few came to ask for the
strength to endure.

* * * * *

At the age of twelve, Pietruccio Cugino (b. 1913–?) a red tint
began to affect his vision. Within five years, he was blind. As a youth,
he helped Padre Pio as best he could in odd jobs. Upon the passing of
Pietruccio's parents, Padre Pio arranged for him to stay in the monastery. This father-son relationship helped nurture the spirituality of
Pietruccio. Within this relationship, Padre Pio asked his young friend
if he was happy. Pietruccio assured him he was. Seeing his content-
ment, Padre Pio asked him if he would like his sight back. Pietruccio
replied, "If to see is useful for the good of my soul, then may the Lord
restore my sight. But if it is harmful to my spiritual salvation, then I
prefer to remain blind."[4] In this choice was the grace of acceptance and
understanding that God was both sanctifying the soul of Pietruccio
and using it to sanctify others. The gain was greater than the pain.

It takes a special soul to remain suffering without bitterness,
understanding the spirituality and power that comes with it. This
only occurs when special graces are given to do so, for we can do

nothing by ourselves. Such a soul understands two things about such a life: they will experience the suffering of Christ's Passion, and Christ will use their suffering to heal others to complete what is lacking in the afflictions of Christ on behalf of His body, which is the church. It is a life lived for Christ where to die for Him is gain. It is a life where pain has clarity and faith. These are the graces that make a Victim Soul.

St. Catherine of Sienna, St. Mother Teresa of Calcutta, St. Faustina of Poland, St. Teresa of Avila, and St. Pio were Victim Souls. These saints not only endured their sufferings without bitterness, they asked God for them for the sake of sinners and to demonstrate their love for Him. In their desire to love Him, He allowed them by His grace a knowledge of His suffering and participation in His Passion. Could we ever live up to their standards? We can only offer to God what He allows in our lives. With a little faith, we may even see their value and ask they not be removed.

Gaicomo Gaglione (1896–1962) came from a well-to-do Italian family. An athletic handsome young man, he came from a wealthy family with many opportunities. An accomplished bicyclist, he led the life of a normal teenager. At the age of sixteen, he began to feel an uneasiness in his feet. Shortly after, his joints and feet began to swell. Within a few weeks, Giacomo was completely paralyzed. His once active life had changed into one of complete dependence on others. Common everyday tasks were now impossible. But his determination to get better kept his spirit up.

At the age of nineteen, he began a relationship with a relative. Eventually, they fell in love and were engaged. The relationship was allowed by the girl's mother, hoping it would help Giacomo get better. But as all realized, he was not improving, and the mother ended the relationship. Giacomo was devastated and fell into a deep depression.

Reading an article on Padre Pio seven years later, he was taken with the healings of the Capuchin monk, and in particular, the hands of Padre Pio that were the source of many healings. Giacomo's hopes of finding healing from Padre Pio lifted his spirits. This reignited the relationship with his former fiancé and again planned to marry.

Giacomo's family resisted taking him to see the stigmatist fearing he would fall deeper into depression if he did not receive the grace of healing. Upon Giacomo's insistence, they agreed. As everyone who wishes to speak with Padre Pio must meet him in the confessional, it would be there that Giacomo planned to ask him for healing. After confession, without Giacomo saying a word, Padre Pio stared at him with an intense deep look. Quietly Giacomo left the confessional without asking for healing. In the silence of the confessional, something changed. Although Giacomo did not ask Padre Pio for healing, the stare had opened his soul to understanding suffering and the purpose of his. He began to see that the stigmatic hands that so captivated him were not only tools of healing, but a source of suffering for Padre Pio. From the moment he left the confessional, he began to see that suffering could be a form of healing for others, that in suffering, a person participates in the Passion of Christ, and in Christ Himself. In the stare of Padre Pio was the intercessory grace of understanding, of pain with clarity and purpose.

Giacomo began to sense a call to participate in the work of salvation through his suffering, that his suffering was the grace from God to do so. As Christ suffered and continues to suffer for the sins of the world, Giacomo would offer his and help make reparation. He no longer wished to be healed, but rather share in the suffering of Christ as Padre Pio did. Giacomo died to self so that Christ could live in him and began to live the life of a Victim Soul.

Giacomo went on to found several Catholic organizations that helped those with physical illnesses accept their sufferings and see the value and worth in them. In 1994, Giacomo Gaglione became Venerable Giacomo Gaglione. Before his death, Giacomo received a telegram from Padre Pio: "*With Jesus on the Cross, with Jesus in Holy Paradise.*"

* * * * *

Once it is known our suffering sanctifies us and can sanctify others, we may, by the grace of God, ask for our pain and suffering to remain. We become living martyrs dying to ourselves, alive in Christ, giving up a temporary need for an eternal reward, to say My suffering is your healing. And great will be our power to intercede as our soul becomes like the Lord's.

No other faith or religion can answer the question better than Catholicism: why does God allow suffering? In Redemptive Suffering, one finds the answer. In Redemptive Suffering, one finds purpose, *even salvation.* If allowed and placed in the hands of Christ, suffering purifies. It purifies in mercy; it purifies in judgment. It brings healing and salvation. In Redemptive Suffering, pain has clarity and purpose when united to the sacrifice of the Cross.

We must carry our cross before we wear our crown. We are purified in our suffering and made to resemble Him. In Baptism, we are born into the Kingdom of God; we live in Christ. In sanctification, we die to self and gain Him. The Victim Soul is the foot soldier in the battle of redemptive suffering. Christ is our guide along "the way of Padre Pio."

In His Own Words

So many come to San Giovanni Rotondo asking for healing. So few ask for the grace to bear their cross.[5]

(How to avoid Purgatory) By accepting everything from God's hands. By offering everything to Him with love and thanksgiving so as to pass from our death-bed to Paradise.[6]

I am happy to suffer with Jesus. In contemplating the Cross on His shoulders, I feel more and more fortified, and I exult with Holy joy.[7]

Jesus chooses souls, and despite my unworthiness, He has chosen mine also to help Him in the tremendous task of men's salvation. This is the whole reason why I desire to suffer.[8]

If God lets you walk on the stormy waters of adversity, do not doubt, do not be afraid. God is with you; have courage, and you will be delivered.[9]

Don't be afraid, for no suffering will go unrewarded in eternal life.[10]

Therefore, undertake your salvation on the Cross. Stretch yourself out on it and be patient with yourself, because, in your patience, as the Divine Master tells us, you will possess your soul. And the less this possession is mixed up with haste and restlessness, the more stable it will be.[11]

In this life Jesus does not ask you to carry the heavy cross with Him, but a small piece of His cross, a piece that consists of human suffering.[12]

We do not want to understand that God neither wants nor is able to save or sanctify us without the cross and the more He draws a soul to Himself, the more He purifies it by means of the cross.[13]

Therefore, don't fear at all, but consider yourself extremely fortunate to have been worthy of participating in the sufferings of the God-Man...resign yourself to drinking the chalice of Gethsemane.[14]

It is not consolations that are needed, but suffering. Aridity, listlessness, helplessness, these are the signs of real love...by suffering we have something to give to God. The gift of our pain, of our suffering is a great thing, which we cannot do in Paradise.[15]

Love Jesus, love Him a lot, but to do this, be ready to love sacrifice more.[16]

If you suffer with resignation in doing His will, you do not offend Him but love Him. And your heart will find great comfort in remembering that in your hour of pain Jesus Himself suffers in you and for you. He did not abandon you when you fled from Him; why should He abandon you now that you are proving your love for Him by the martyrdom of your soul?[17]

Bearing physical and moral ailments is the worthiest offering you can make to He who saved us through suffering.[18]

Accept all suffering and incomprehension that comes from Above. In this way you will perfect and sanctify yourself.[19]

To God we owe all our love, which, to be adequate, ought to be infinite… We must at least give our whole being to love, to charity… To carry out this deal of our Lord, we must be quite forgetful of self. Rising above selfishness, we must bow down to the sufferings and the wounds of our fellow men. We must make them our own, knowing how to suffer with our brethren for the love of God. We must know how to instill hope into their hearts and bring back a smile to their lips, having restored a ray of light into their souls. Then we shall be offering God the most beautiful, the most noble of prayers, because our prayers will have sprung from sacrifice.[20]

[1] Pio, I am consumed by love for God.
[2] Benincasa, p. 9.
[3] Ibid, p. 9.
[4] Ruffin, pp. 389–390.
[5] Allen, 2011, p. 312.
[6] Parente, 2015, pp. 62–63.
[7] Pio, 1999, p. 97.
[8] Ibid, p. 97.
[9] Ibid, p. 158.
[10] Ibid, p. 160.
[11] Ibid, p. 49.
[12] Pio, 2018, p. 45.
[13] Ibid., p. 44.
[14] Ibid., pp. 46–47.
[15] Ibid., p. 49
[16] Ibid., p. 50
[17] Ibid., p. 52
[18] Ibid., p. 57
[19] Ibid., p. 58
[20] Allen, 2011, pp. 66–67.

Penance and Reparation

When Padre Pio learned a woman was doing harsh penances on herself, he replied, "There are many ways to do penance, such as offering to the Lord whatever trouble comes to us day by day. It's up to the Lord to give us our cross."[1]

Penance expresses sorrow; reparation expresses the desire to make it right. In her book, *Pray, Hope, and Don't Worry,* Diane Allen records a story of Giovanni da Prato, an Italian taxi driver, whose life changes forever after meeting Padre Pio in a dream. The extent of the change and how it was achieved through penance and reparation makes it noteworthy here.

Giovanni was two things before meeting Padre Pio, a communist and an alcoholic. The second was the cause of his wife's constant beating which warranted a visit from Padre Pio through bi-location, whose visit was brought upon by the prayers of the wife. Giovanni's curiosity got the better of him, and he drove to see Padre Pio but was chased away. Although Padre Pio would not see Giovanni, the stigmata priest would continue intercession for him, eventually turning Giovanni's heart to God, upon which Padre Pio saw him for confession. Giovanni wanted to turn his life around and started by giving his Communist party card to Padre Pio. Padre Pio was pleased and added that he needed to make reparation for all those he hurt while in the party.

The heart and soul of Giovanni da Prato was ready to repent and show remorse for his former life without God. Padre Pio told Giovanni to attend the last Sunday Mass of the day. The rules for attendance then were much different and stricter than today. The rule for receiving Communion was to fast from the last meal of the day before receiving the Host the next day. For Giovanni, that meant every Sunday, he could not eat until he received Communion at the last Mass.

In our day, such a penance would not only be difficult, but it would be impracticable. For almost a year, Giovanni did as he was told. In that time, his words changed. He prayed the Rosary, and he stopped drinking. When he told Padre Pio he was having trouble with a few bad habits, St. Pio told him, "Giovanni, you put in your good will, and I will take care of the rest of it."[2]

The acts of penance and reparation in the case of Giovanni da Prato were not only born out of sorrow and remorse, they were life changing. In the end, they resulted in a love for the Creator of his soul. For us, what will they mean?

Penance and Reparation

The acts of *penance* and *reparation* offer both the one praying and the one being prayed for the *purification of soul*. The greatest act and foundation for reparation and expiation of sin is the sacrifice of the Mass. Therefore, every act of penance and reparation must be united to the sacrifice of the Mass. It is the standard for expiation and forgiveness. Without this, the soul is under the Old Law and judged by it. St. Faustina tells us why:

> God will refuse me nothing when I entreat
> Him with the voice of His Son. My sacrifice is
> nothing in itself, but when I join it to the sacri-
> fice of Jesus Christ, it becomes all-powerful, and
> has the power to appease divine wrath.[3]

The finite is immersed into the Infinite. It is the infinite value of love that gives value to the finite act of suffering when we join it to the sacrifice of Jesus Christ. Only the Infinite can appease the Infinite.

The *prayer of penance* shows *sorrow* and *remorse* on behalf of the penitent; the *act of reparation* offers to *amend a wrong*—often performed with great difficulty and pain, to demonstrate the sincerity and sorrow of the act for which the reparation is offered.

In granting St. Faustina a request for the conversion of others, Jesus said, "Every conversion of a sinful soul demands sacrifice."[4] This tells us the need for and value of sacrifice. Sacrifice is expressed through penance and reparation.

The sacrifice of reparation and penance through suffering, united to the Sacrifice of the Mass, through the power of the Holy Spirit, enables our suffering to have meaning, clarity, and purpose. These acts sanctify ourselves and others. They not only compensate for the sin. They alter the nature that caused it, through self-denial, thereby, purifying the will and uniting it to God. Jesus, using the act of sacrifice, explained the difference between *knowing* about His Passion and *participating* in it as a way to participate in His nature.

As St. Faustina was suffering in her obedience, Jesus told her, "But when your mind is dimmed and your sufferings are great, it is then that you take an active part in My Passion, and I am conforming you more fully to Myself."[5] Suffering absorbs us into the very being of God whereby our bodies become His and our souls belong completely to Him. As He bore our guilt and expiated it through suffering, so we can, in our suffering, help Him rescue souls from sin. This is why Jesus said to St. Faustina, "I have need of your sufferings to rescue souls."[6] Our suffering, united to His, completes what is lacking in the afflictions of Christ on behalf of His body, which is the church (Colossians 1:24). Such is the cornerstone of penance and reparation when united to His suffering on the Cross.

Penance

When we offer penance for our sins, we offer remorse. In the act of reconciliation, confession, we bring our sins committed in darkness into the light. We place them on the altar before God and acknowledge our sin. This is the beginning of healing and cleansing of the soul. St. Pio told one penitent that although the saint knew his sins, the penitent still had to confess them. He also told his children to attend confession every eight days. He knew the value and importance of confession so much he spent two-thirds of the day at it.

A god-fearing spiritual director is a great grace from God. Without the confessor God gave to St. Faustina, she could not have completed the work He gave her to do. Jesus explained to her,

> And now I am going to tell you something that is most important for you: boundless sincerity with your spiritual director. If you do not take advantage of this grace according to My instructions, I will take him away from you, and then you will be left to yourself and all the torments, which you know very well, will return to you. It displeases Me that you do not take advantage of the opportunity when you are able to see him and talk with him. Know that it is a great grace on My part when I give a spiritual director to a soul.[7]

The church understands its importance and has penitential days we are to observe:

> The Divine Law binds all the Christian faithful to do penance each in his or her own way. In order for all to be united among themselves by some common observance of penance, however, penitential days are prescribed on which the Christian faithful devote themselves in a special way to prayer, perform works of piety and charity, and deny themselves by fulfilling their own obligations more faithfully and especially by observing fast and abstinence, according to the norm of the Canon.[8] (Code of Canon Law: Chapter 2: 1249)

The sorrow (a form of suffering) we show in penance is expressed in the act of reparation, the degree we are willing to make things right. This pays the debt of sin. This is the standard God set when He degreed that only the Cross could save. Penance brings forgiveness and expiation through the sorrow we feel for our sin. This begins to alter the sinful nature that caused the act and brings us into His likeness. If penance brings forgiveness, reparation brings purification.

Reparation

Reparation is an act of sacrifice offered to God to make amends for an offense. The value of the sacrifice we offer as reparation for our sin is expressed in the degree of suffering we give to Christ. The reparation can be for ourselves, or another. Reparations help to mortify our self-will, to purify us and bring us closer to Him. The act causes us to come out of ourselves, to deny our will and seek His. We offer reparation for the *sorrow* we feel for our past behavior and the need to make it right. In our desire to be closer to Him or to help another, we offer a sacrifice as an offering to intensify a request made and to amend a wrong. We seek to purify our soul in light of His holiness through these sacrifices. A reparation is a sacrifice.

> Daughter, I need sacrifice lovingly accomplished because that alone has meaning for Me. Enormous indeed are the debts of the world... pure souls can pay them by their sacrifice, exercising mercy in spirit.[9] (Jesus to St. Faustina)

Acts of reparation relieve us of self-will and allow Christ to enter and, thereby, sanctify us. The sanctification of soul brings power and strength to our prayer of intercession.

> I have granted the grace you asked for on behalf of that soul, but not because of the mortification you choose for yourself. Rather, it was because of your act of complete obedience to

> My representative that I granted this grace to that soul for whom you interceded and begged mercy. Know that when you mortify your own self-will, then Mine reigns within you.[10] (Jesus to St. Faustina)

These acts of reparation strive against our sinful nature: anger, impatience, lack of faith, distrust, desires of the flesh, etc. They obtain for us the graces needed to remove all that is not of the Father from our lives. They are our cross we must pick up daily. "Just as the body needs nourishment, so does the soul need the cross, day after day, to purify it and detach it from creatures"[11] (Padre Pio).

Acts of reparation can include fasting, rising early to pray and read scripture, completing a deed of charity for a person we do not care for, praying for someone God has placed on our hearts, attending reconciliation monthly, daily Mass, volunteering for a position at church, or attending adoration, and of course, praying the Rosary. Reparation is as different as the person completing it. Remember, the greater the sacrifice (reparation), the purer the love, the greater the power to intercede.

> My daughter, I want to instruct you on how you are to rescue souls through *sacrifice and prayer*. You will save more souls through *prayer and suffering* than will a missionary through his teachings and sermons alone. I want to see you as a sacrifice of living love, which only then carries weight before Me… And great will be your power for whomever you intercede.[12] (Italics mine)

Suffering, pain, sacrifice—we cannot escape these undeniable virtues. They are weapons against sin when united to the sacrifice of the Cross; freely given, they empower Christ to move in our lives and others.

When and Where

There are two areas in our life where penance and reparation can be found—in the daily living of life and in the suffering God allows.

God, in His providence, has provided the means for our sanctification through penance and reparation. We learn to use life and its circumstances for His glory and our salvation. In doing so, we begin to remove from our lives all that is not of the Father. Remember, everything has eternal value.

In living the daily "stuff of life," we offer to Him what comes our way. It is the little stuff God uses to make us His. We learn to look more closely at what we do, think, and say as everything becomes an offering: heavy morning traffic making us late to work, unruly neighbors, a burned dinner, running late to pick up a child from school, an employer who has acted unfairly. These events come to us as "the stuff of life," the providence of God.

They *can* be offered as a daily sacrifice. You can take it with you—if it is done in His love, in His will.

> Here is a rule for life: Do not do anything
> which you cannot offer to God.[13] (St. Vianney)

In the second area, where God brings trial and suffering into our life, He has a heavenly purpose. He would make us in His image.

> The trial to which God the Father has subjected you is not a punishment for your unfaithfulness. This is not so, I repeat, for he has forgotten everything. The trial has been sent to you in order to make you a more and more worthy bride of His beloved Son. This harsh trial is offered to you to enable you to collect more and more prizes and crowns to be presented to your Spouse when you are united with Him in Heaven.[14] (St. Pio)

> Rest assured that the more a soul is pleas-
> ing to God, the more it must be tried. Therefore,
> courage, and go forward.[15] (St. Pio)

These trials are often the hardest, most difficult to get through as they get to the heart of our soul. As in the life of Job, they often involve those things most close and valuable to us: family, home, social position, body and health, finances and death. They are the means of sanctification. They are His hand in our life that circumcise the heart (Deuteronomy 30:6).

> Pain and suffering have come into your life,
> but remember, pain, sorrow, suffering are but the
> Kiss of Jesus—a sign that you have come so close
> to Him that He can kiss you.[16] (Mother Teresa)

These are the trials where we ask others to pray for us. It is the time we battle Satan for our faith, where we say in our pain, "Though He slay me, yet will I trust Him" (Job 13:15). But they also offer us greater sanctification and greater glory to God; therefore, the greater the suffering, the greater the value, the greater the sanctification, the purer the love, the greater the reflection of Christ in us.

> Then we shall be offering God the most
> beautiful, the most noble prayers, because our
> prayer will have sprung from sacrifice.[17] (Padre
> Pio)

It is here we offer the most powerful intercession for another because we offer up our pain with it. *We wrap our suffering around the soul of the other, unite it to the suffering of God, and offer us both to the Lord for healing.* It is an opportunity for others to embrace our pain as well. The Victim Souls take on much more. Padre Pio, upon receiving a sick man, quietly prayed, "Oh God, there is so much suffering, so much sickness. Please take away the sufferings of that poor man and give them to me."[18]

Interceding for one another through penance and reparation, we become a community of reparable souls.

How Should We Then Live?

Suffering is natural; it is constant. It occurs in life alongside joy and happiness. God is the author of both.

> Consider the work of God; who can make straight what he has made crooked? On a good day, enjoy good things, and on an evil day consider: Both the one and the other God has made, so that man cannot find fault with Him. (Ecclesiastes 7:13–14)

All suffering can be offered to our Lord. Suffering offered as penance or reparation may be on behalf of a loved one, as well as the purification of our own soul. We offer these acts of penance and reparation to the degree they have meaning for us or to the degree we wish to sacrifice for another. Our place is to open ourselves to His guidance so that *how* we live our lives can be used to help others live theirs. Whatever pain comes to us through the tempting of Satan, the daily stuff of life, or what we freely offer to Him, we can be more than conquerors in Him who is able to carry us through it all.

At Fatima, Mary taught the children this prayer to be said before offering any thought or action, thereby giving it meaning and purpose: "O Jesus, it is for You, for the love of sinners, and in reparation for the sins committed against the Immaculate Heart of Mary"[19] (Our Lady of Fatima).

The saints continue with their guidance on living the redemptive life.

> Your weeping has power over Me and the pain in your desire binds Me like a chain.[20] (St. Catherine of Siena)

> Every suffering they bear from any source…
> is of infinite worth, and so satisfies the offer that
> deserved infinite penalty.[21] (St. Catherine of Siena)

> You are not living for yourself but for souls,
> and other souls will profit from your suffer-
> ings. Your prolonged suffering will give them
> light and strength to accept My will.[22] (Jesus to
> St. Faustina)

In living the redemptive life, we can say with Mother Teresa,

> Jesus, I accept whatever You give, and I give
> whatever You take.[23]

Whatever your pain, whether it comes from "the stuff of life," or a suffering He has allowed into your life, we are more than conquerors.

Jesus, speaking to St. Catherine of Siena, explained why there is pain, temptation, and strife:

> My love permits these temptations, for the
> Devil is weak. He can do nothing by himself
> unless I allow him. So, let him tempt you because
> I love you, not because I hate you. I want you
> to conquer, not to be conquered, and to come
> to a perfect knowledge of yourself and Me.[24] (St.
> Catherine of Siena)

* * * * *

The sufferings of Padre Pio came from many sources. They came from the daily stuff of life, from his intercession for others, from the church hierarchy, and from his wounds of Christ. They came as he offered himself in the Mass as a sacrifice for others. They came from the trials God sent his way. They came because he asked for them. They came because God needed a soul who would love Him more than his own pain and would offer that pain as reparation for the healing and conversion of sinners and as expiation for sins committed against the Immaculate Heart of Mary.

We walk "the way of Padre Pio" when we offer and accept the sufferings and trials of life. We live the redemptive life when through our sufferings, we make reparation for others who cannot make it for themselves through the blindness of sin in their lives. We receive power to do this when we unite ourselves to His Passion as His victims through penance and reparation. This is "the way of Padre Pio."

* * * * *

In His Own Words

O God, show Yourself more and more to this poor heart of mine, and complete in me the work You have begun. I hear deep within me, a voice which says to me repeatedly—sanctify yourself and sanctify others.[25]

It is the Lord who works within you, and you must do nothing except leave the door of your heart wide open so that He may work as He pleases.[26]

Oh Jesus, save everyone; I offer myself as a victim for everyone; strengthen me, take my heart, fill it with Your love and then command me to do whatever You want.[27]

We do not want to understand that God neither wants nor is able to save or sanctify us without the cross, and the more He draws a soul to Himself, the more he purifies it by means of the cross.[28]

1 Ruffin, p. 343.
2 Allen, 2011, p.203.
3 Michalenko, p. 110 (#482).
4 Ibid, p. 163 (#961).
5 Ibid, p. 257 (#1697).
6 Ibid, p. 242, (#1612).
7 Ibid, p. 233 (#1561).
8 Code of Canon Law
9 Michalenko, p. 197 (#1316).
10 Kowalska, p. 164 (#365).
11 Pio, 2018, p. 44.
12 Kowalska. p. 627 (#1767).
13 Vianney, p.5.
14 Pio, 1999, p. 119.
15 Pio, 2018, p. 70.
16 Teresa, p. 281.
17 Allen, 2011, p. 67.
18 Ibid, p. 62.
19 McGlynn, p. 204.
20 Benincasa, p. 27.
21 Ibid, p. 4.
22 Michalenko, p. 39 (#67).
23 Teresa, p. 225.
24 Thigpen, p. 160.
25 Allen, 2012, p. 363.
26 Pio, 1999, p. 70.
27 Pio, 2018, p. 122.
28 Ibid, p. 44.

The Way of Padre Pio

O God, show Yourself more and more to this poor
heart of mine, and complete in me the work You have
begun. I hear deep within me, a voice which says to me
repeatedly—sanctify yourself and sanctify others.[1]

—Padre Pio

Mary Pyle, in a letter to a friend, wrote,

> When your children want explanations
> about Padre Pio, just tell them that he loves Jesus
> so much, and Jesus loves him so much, that they
> have become very much alike. Jesus has given
> Padre Pio His wounds, so that they can both suf-
> fer together to make us all be good.[2]

How can one be so close to Jesus one would take on His wounds?
If so, how do you begin such a task?

C. Bernard Ruffin, in his biography of Padre Pio, *Padre Pio: The True Story*, compiled a list of ten guidelines for living the Christian life. These guidelines were St. Pio's spiritual principles born out of his battles with Satan, his own temptations, his conversations with

Jesus, Mary, and the saints, and his life in the spirit world. They are "the way of Padre Pio."

1. *Put your trust in Christ as your personal Savior.*

> This heart of mine is Yours…my Jesus, so take this heart of mine, fill it with Your love and then order me to do whatever You wish.[3] (Padre Pio)

It is not enough to believe there is a God. The devil knows and trembles but will not humble himself before God. We must humble ourselves before the Cross if we wish to be the person God wants us to be. There is no other way to the Father. "Jesus said to him, 'I am the way and the truth and the life. No one comes to the Father except through me'" (John 14:6). In all things, acknowledge Him, and He will direct your paths.

2. *Realize that you have no righteousness of your own.*

> The Scripture says that we of ourselves cannot say the name of Jesus except through the action of the Holy Spirit.[4] (Padre Pio)

St. Paul wrote in Romans 7:18, "For I know that good does not dwell in me, that is, in my flesh. The willing is ready at hand, but doing the good is not." We can do nothing of ourselves. Even in this simple task of seeking Him, it is not within us to do so. We struggle with this through distractions of living life. If we desire to seek Him, it is because we have allowed God to move us. Our simple *yes* is His permission to work in us.

Unless we realize that all have sinned and come short of the glory of God, we cannot be saved. It must be by the grace of God that our eyes and heart open. This act must come from God. Padre Pio, in all his holiness, claimed, "What can I do? Everything comes from God."[5]

Without the grace to see Him, we are blind to His presence as Mary Magdalene was when He rose from His tomb Resurrection morning. It was only when He said her name did she know it was Him.

3. *Beware of the devil and resist him.*

> The field of battle between God and Satan is the human soul. This is where it takes place every moment of our lives.[6] (Padre Pio)

Satan's power lies in his ability to remain unacknowledged. In this, he is able to disguise himself in media, music, science, and even religion. Of His purpose, St. Catherine of Siena writes the words Jesus gave her,

> I have appointed the devil to tempt and to trouble My creatures in this life. I have done this, not so My creatures will be overcome, but so that they may overcome, proving their virtue and receiving from Me the glory of victory.[7]

He continues,

> My love permits these temptations, for the Devil is weak. He can do nothing by himself unless I allow him. I let him tempt you because I love you, not because I hate you. I want you to conquer, not to be conquered, and to come to a perfect knowledge of yourself and of Me.[8]

Padre Pio warns us of Satan's presence and hold in our lives. "There are so many (devils) that if each one wanted to assume a body as small as a grain of sand, they would block out the sun."[9] The power lies not in their number but in the power we give them. "The devil has only one door through which to enter into our soul: the will. The devil is like a raging dog on a chain; outside the limit of the chain he can bite no one."[10]

We are no match for Satan. He has had thousands of years to perfect his trade. He is patient, the Hound of Hell.

4. *Pray to God and say, in every circumstance, "Thy will be done."*

> You cannot win the battle without prayer.[11]
> (Padre Pio)

> Prayer is the effusion of our heart into God's…when it is done well, it moves the Divine Heart and makes Him always more inclined to grant our requests.[12] (Padre Pio)

Through prayer and in life's circumstances, we say I surrender *my will to You*. In doing so, we allow Him to work through us, with us, and *in us* to accomplish His will.

Father Dolindo Routolo (1882–1970), of which Padre Pio said, "The whole of paradise is in your soul,"[13] was given by Jesus the *Novena of Surrender to the Will of God.* Consisting of nine days, each day of the novena moves one to surrender to the Father's will and relinquish all circumstances to Him. "O Jesus, I surrender myself to You. Take care of everything."[14] These words convey complete surrender of mind, body, and soul with the faith He will do what is best.

Jesus said to Father Routolo,

> If you say to Me truly: "Thy will be done,"
> which is the same as saying, "You take care of it,"
> I will intervene with all My omnipotence, and I
> will resolve the most difficult situations. By My
> love, I promise you this.[15]

Can the will of God change? In an interview with a fellow priest, Ruffin shares of Padre Pio, "He expressed his belief that some things are degreed from eternity, but other things depend upon the prayers of human beings."[16] Padre Pio himself tells us, "It is true that God's power triumphs over everything, but humble and suffering prayer prevails over God Himself."[17]

Offer yourself in prayer and suffering *constantly* that He may *use you* to fulfill His will in the lives of those you pray for.

5. *Love the Cross.*

> Yes, I love the Cross, the Cross alone; I love
> it because I see it always on Jesus' shoulders.[18]
> (Padre Pio)

The Cross cannot be separated from who Jesus is. It is the standard of His love; it defines His love for us. Jesus came to us for one purpose, to offer Himself as a sacrifice for humanity and atone for its sins. It allows us to come to the Father's throne without sin by accepting His substitution for us on the Cross, for nothing sinful can approach God. God the Father has deemed suffering as the only payment for sin. *Suffering cleanses sin.* It purges the nature that created the sin (e.g., purgatory). The Cross did just that. God desires us to be like Him in nature and deed. It begins with the acceptance of the Cross and continues with the acceptance of suffering in our lives, by way of the Cross.

St. Pio reminds us of this: "He wants you to be similar to Him in the anguish of the desert, the Garden and on the Cross."[19] With each acceptance of our "desert, garden, and cross," united to the sacrifice of Christ, we allow His Spirit to enter our lives and become Christlike. We deny our will and accept His.

Our journey becomes our desire to live in His Passion, to live in His will. St. Pio continues, "Every soul that wants to be saved must undergo something of that mysterious storm because every predestined soul must resemble Jesus."[20] We do not let our suffering define us. Instead, it molds us into the person He wants us to be. Every cross, no matter how big or small, brings us closer to God. Every sliver sanctifies. Before the crown, there must be the cross. This leads us to the next task.

6.   *Offer every action up to God.*

> Do not start any activity without first offering it to God.[21] (Padre Pio)

In offering everything to God, by placing all things in His Hands, we consecrate all things to Him and thereby give it eternal value. If you cannot offer an act to God, perhaps it is not an act to do. The acts we offer should unite us to Jesus and make us more like Him. St. Pio wrote in one of his letters, "Physical and spiritual ills are the most worthy offering you can make to Him who saved you by suffering."[22]

Every action, offered to God, has redemptive and eternal value and will sanctify both the self and those it is offered for. St. Pio tells us the value of all we do:

> And yet, we must give an exact account
> of every moment, of every grace, of every holy
> inspiration, of every opportunity to do good.
> The slightest transgression of God's holy laws,
> will be taken into consideration![23]

When an act is placed in His Hands, consecrated to Him, it is out of reach of Satan. He cannot touch nor desecrate it and use it against us. If unsure of the act, ask the Father, Mary, and the saints to remove anything that is not of the Father from the act. When offering a sacrifice or suffering, begin with the Prayer of Fatima:

> O Jesus, it is for Your love, for the conversion
> of sinners, and in reparation for the sins committed against the Immaculate heart of Mary.[24]

7. *Never worry.*

> Beware of anxiety and restlessness because there is nothing that more greatly impedes progress towards perfection.[25] (Padre Pio)

Many saints in Scripture were given promises by God. Before fulfilling them, Satan was allowed to tempt them. A period of dryness and aridity, of silent dark nights, was allowed to disbelieve the promises of God and doubt His love. These times of silence are times of trust and purification. Their purpose is to place our desires in Him, not in His blessings. They remove all that is us to be replaced with all that is Him. They purify and remove what is weak in our faith. These times are allowed not that we may be overcome, but that we may overcome the world.

When God declares a goodness in your life, followed by His silence, trust in His love for you. Worry shows a lack of trust, which greatly offends God. It hinders the work of the Holy Spirit in our lives. Worry is a focus on us; faith is a focus on Him. When you offer your love and faith to Him, He must purify them in the circumstances that test them, until all that is left is His will. The purity of saying, *I trust You*, is refined in the fire of trial. Jesus said to St. Catherine of Siena explaining to her the goal of faith, "Their own will lost, they clothe themselves in Mine, and I will nothing but your sanctification."[26]

Ultimately, when the soul submits itself to Him and,

> Infirmity, or poverty, or change of worldly condition, or loss of children, or of other much-loved creatures…come upon them, they endure them all with the light of reason and holy faith, looking to Me, who am the Supreme Good, and who cannot desire other than good, for which I permit these tribulations through love, and not through hatred.[27]

In preparation for what was to come, Jesus told St. Faustina,

> Be watchful that you lose no opportunity that My providence offers you for sanctification. If you do not succeed in taking advantage of an opportunity (for sanctification), do not lose your peace, but, humble yourself profoundly before Me, and, with great trust, immerse yourself completely in My mercy. In this way, you gain more than you have lost, because more favor is granted to a humble soul than the soul itself asks for.[28]

Don't worry. Pray for strength through the intercession of Padre Pio, Mother Mary, and the saints. In the end, there is peace. "Wherefore, the will not being there, neither is there any pain. They bear everything with reverence, deeming themselves favored in having tribulation for My sake, and they desire nothing but what I desire"[29] (Jesus to St. Catherine of Siena). Remember, through the Immaculate Heart of Mary, the battle is already won. In the end, there is what He causes, what He prevents, and what He allows. In His Hands, it is all for our sanctification (Romans 8:28–29).

In His Own Words

> Pray, hope and don't worry. Worry [sic] is useless. God is merciful and will hear your prayer.[30]

> Therefore, if any thought agitates you, this agitation never comes from God, who gives you peace, being the Spirit of Peace, but from the devil.[31]

> If we are calm and patient, we will not only find ourselves, but also our souls and, with it, God.[32]

Patience is more perfect when it is less mixed
up with worries and disturbances.[33]

The spirit of the devil, instead, excites, exasperates and makes us feel, in that very sorrow,
anger against ourselves.[34]

You are suffering, but believe, also, that
Jesus is suffering within you, with you, and for
you.[35]

8.   *Aspire to the heavenly prize.*

No suffering, no matter how low the motive
on which it rests, will go unrewarded in eternal
life.[36] (Padre Pio)

We live in this world, but hope in the next. Our hope is where
our loved ones are who have passed. Of a child who had died, St.
Pio said, "Your child is in paradise, watching over you, assisting you,
smiling on you, and preparing a place for you."[37] He added, "Heaven
is total joy, continuous joy."[38]

For where your treasure is, there also will be
your heart. (Luke 12:34)

9.   *Love the Madonna.*

Some people are so foolish that they think
they can go through life without the help of the
Blessed Mother.[39] (Padre Pio)

"When a woman asked, 'Teach me a shortcut to reach God
quickly,' St. Pio answered, 'The shortcut…is the Virgin… She is the
perfect example of God's mercy and acts as His double.'"[40] Gabriel
Amorth, chief exorcist for the Vatican, said of a demon during an

exorcism, "Every Hail Mary is like a blow on my head. If Christians knew how powerful the Rosary was, it would be my end."[41] St. Bonaventure wrote, "Men do not fear a powerful, hostile army as much as the powers of hell fear the name and protection of Mary."[42]

As St. Pio and another Capuchin observed an elderly priest praying his Rosary, Padre Pio commented,

> Do you see Brother Costantino? Old and sick as he is, he seems now to be worth nothing. And yet, as an obedient son of Holy Mother Church, who knows how to hold a Rosary in his hand, and knows how to pray to the Madonna, he is worth more than you or me. Do you know why he has so much peace of soul? Because he has placed all his trust in the Most Holy Virgin, and because he interests himself as little as possible in the problems of the world. His spirit of prayer and his devotion to the Most Holy Virgin are virtues that wash away all defects and all human weaknesses. He draws on himself the gaze of the Madonna and his prayers have saved many souls… I would almost say that she gets her strength from the prayers of these men whom you consider worthless.[43]

Padre Pio died as he lived—with his rosary in his hand saying, "Jesus, Mary."

In His Own Words

She is the Mediatrix of all graces.[44]

Let us always love this Mother more and more, and let us be confident that She shall not deny us anything because to Her nothing is lacking, and She has the heart of a Mother and a Queen.[45]

Love the Madonna, and make Her loved. Always recite Her Rosary. That is the armor against the evils of the world today.[46]

Satan wants to destroy this prayer, but in this, he will never succeed. The Rosary is the prayer of those who triumph over everything and everyone. It was Our Lady who taught us this prayer, just as it was Jesus who taught us the Our Father.[47]

10. *Rejoice in the Lord*

Serve the Lord with laughter.[48]

Our hope is that God will not abandon us to this world. In this hope is our joy. Joy lies in the hope we will see our loved ones again who have passed on; joy lies in the belief our pain has value and redemption, that with it we can help others in their journey to God. Joy lies in the knowledge we will see the face of God and the security we are carved onto the palm of His Hand. Our hope is our joy.

* * * * *

The spiritual children of Padre Pio understand the importance of his spirituality—of becoming so close to Jesus they can share His wounds—and help those they pray for. Yet his wounds were not the totality of his existence. His spirituality was more than suffering for others; there was his offering and participation in the Mass, his love for the Eucharist, his need for confession and constant prayer to our beloved Madonna. It was living through Jesus, with Jesus, and in Jesus, even in his dark night. This must be our spirituality, our daily living, to sanctify ourselves and sanctify others. And as we do, perhaps we will meet the person God wants us to be along *the way*.

* * * * *

Priest: "Padre, will we contemplate you crucified in Paradise?"
Padre Pio: "For your greater glory."[49]

---

1   Allen, 2012, p.363.
2   Ibid, p. 173.
3   Pio, 2018, p. 168.
4   Ruffin, p. 173.
5   Pio, 2018, p. 157.
6   Ibid, p. 99.
7   Thigpen, p. 159.
8   Ibid, p. 160.
9   Ruffin, p. 173.
10 Pio, 2018, p. 74.
11 Ibid, p. 36.
12 Pio, 2018, p. 23.
13 Ruotolo, pp. 268–269.
14 Novena of Surrender to the Will of God Prayer.
15 Ibid.
16 Ruffin, p. 174.
17 Ibid, p. 174.
18 Pio, 2018, p. 54.
19 Ibid. p. 63.
20 Pio, 1999, p. 174.
21 Epistolario, p. 450.
22 Ruffin, p. 176.
23 Pio, 2018, p. 7.
24 McGlynn, p. 204.
25 Ibid, p. 184.
26 Benincasa, p. 68.
27 Ibid, p. 69.
28 Michalenko, p. 201 (#1361).
29 Benincasa, p. 69.
30 Pio, 2018, p. 24.
31 Ibid, p. 200.
32 Ibid, p. 200.

[33] Ibid, p. 201.
[34] Ibid, p. 199.
[35] Ibid, p. 193.
[36] Ruffin, p. 177.
[37] Ibid, p. 176.
[38] Ibid, p.176.
[39] Allen, 2012, p. 33.
[40] Ruffin, p. 177.
[41] Thigpen, p. 236.
[42] Ibid, p. 28.
[43] Allen, 2012, pp. 34.
[44] Ibid, p. 32.
[45] Ibid, p. 44.
[46] Ibid, p. 49.
[47] Ibid, p. 33.
[48] Ruffin, p. 177.
[49] da Cervinara, p. 46.

The Mass

The Mass gives God infinite glory.[1]

—Padre Pio

As a young boy, I sat in the pews during Mass wondering what the words being said meant. I often wondered if anyone else knew. Not knowing the meaning of the Mass, I still participated. I stood when everyone stood, sat when everyone sat, and knelt when everyone knelt. Today, I know the words being said were Latin. And if I heard them today, I would know only a few. This was my Catholic youth. As time moved on, I left the Catholic Church not understanding the Mass, only that Jesus died for my sins.

Perhaps if I had attended a Mass of Padre Pio, I might have had a different view growing up. I had fallen into the trap of "visiting" Jesus in the Mass the same way I would visit my grandparents—out of obligation with some devotion. I was putting in my time.

Today, I participate in the Mass as a lector, Eucharistic minister, and sacristan with a different focus, a new perspective. I *know* Jesus died for my sins, and the Mass celebrates this sacrifice. Each movement has purpose; every word expresses meaning. I bow before Eternal God who sacrifices Himself in the Mass and pronounce the words, "My Lord and my God." I understand the graces I receive when I participate in the Mass. I understand the bread and wine become the Real Presence of Jesus Christ. I fulfill the commandment to eat His flesh and drink His blood which brings me graces to continually live out the Christian life.

* * * * *

The Saints knew the value of the Mass and had much to say about it.

Saint John Vianney:

> All good works together are not of equal value with the Sacrifice of the Mass because they are the works of men, and the holy Mass is the work of God.[2]

> Martyrdom is nothing in comparison; it is the sacrifice that man makes of his life to God; Mass is the sacrifice that God makes to man of His Body and His Blood.[3]

Saint Faustina Kowalska:

> The courage and strength that are in me are not of me, but of Him who lives in me—it is the Eucharist.[4]

> When my strength begins to fail, it is Holy Communion that will sustain me and give me strength. I fear the day on which I would not receive Holy Communion. My soul draws astonishing strength from Holy Communion.[5]

> The most solemn moment of my life is the moment when I receive Holy Communion. I long for each Holy Communion, and for every Holy Communion I give thanks to the most Holy

Trinity. If the angels were capable of envy, they would envy us for two things: one is the receiving of Holy Communion, and the other is suffering.[6]

I desire to unite Myself with human souls; My great delight is to unite Myself with souls. My daughter, that when I come to a human heart in Holy Communion, My hands are full of all kinds of graces which I want to give to the soul. But, souls do not even pay attention to Me; they leave Me to Myself and busy themselves with other things. Oh, how sad I am that souls do not recognize Love! They treat Me as a dead object.[7] (Jesus to St. Faustina)

Virgin Mary to Blessed Mary of Agreda from the *Mystical City of God.*

Oh, my daughter! Would that the believers in the holy Catholic Faith opened their hardened and stony hearts in order in order to attain to a true understanding of the sacred and mysterious blessing of the holy Eucharist![8]

In this, the happy age of the law of grace, mortals have no reason to complain of their weakness and their passions; since in this bread of heaven they have at hand strength and health. It matters not that they are tempted and persecuted by the demon; for by receiving this sacrament frequently they are able to overcome him gloriously. The faithful are themselves to blame for all their poverty and labors, since they pay no attention to this divine mystery, nor avail themselves of the divine powers, thus placed at their disposal by my most holy Son... Lucifer and his demons have such a fear of the most Holy

Eucharist, that to approach it, causes them more torments than to remain in hell itself. Although they do enter churches in order to tempt souls, they enter them with aversion, forcing themselves to endure cruel pains in the hope of destroying a soul and drawing it into sin, especially in the holy places and in the presence of the holy Eucharist.[9]

The demons fear the souls, who receive the Lord worthily and devotedly and who strive to preserve themselves in this purity until the next Communion.[10]

Moreover, the essential glory of those, who have worthily and devotedly received the holy Eucharist, will in several respects exceed the glory of the many martyrs who have not received the Body and Blood of the Lord.[11]

Mother Mary spoke of consuming the Host and Blood:

I did not consider myself worthy of this one favor.[12]

* * * * *

The Mass is both past and present: the remembrance of the Last Supper, the offering of the Lamb and Its sacrifice, with the actual presence of Christ in the Eucharist renewing His offer to redeem us. The Mass is His commitment to be present in our lives.

Through the representative of Christ—the Priest, following the succession of Peter—Christ speaks the words He spoke at the Last Supper. Cardinal Joseph Ratzinger, later to be Pope Benedict XVI, writes:

In order that an event that occurred in the past is made present, the words must therefore be pronounced: This is My Body—this is My Blood… Only He can say these things; they are His words."[13]

The Mass is where man meets God at Calvary. It is the fulfillment of expiation, the offering of the Sacrificial Lamb where we consume Its flesh and drink Its blood in acceptance of the offering. It is the renewing of our soul. It is both a sad and joyous occasion—the acceptance by the Father of His Son's death in place of ours and the cleansing of our soul whereby we can stand before the throne unblemished. It is where Christ *continues* to offer Himself as expiation for our sin. The Mass fulfills His promise to be with us.

It is a place where I offer myself and those I pray for to the Father. When we speak our intentions, we lay them on the altar for the Father to bestow His graces. All intentions offered say, "The sacrifice of this Mass is for (your intention), for healing, for protection, guidance, and conversion." The Mass is the power by which God the Father shows His mercy and forgiveness.

It is in the offertory I offer myself, where I unite myself to the Sacrifice of the Mass. At the Presentation of the Gifts when the priest says, "Pray, brethren, that my sacrifice and yours may be acceptable to God, the almighty Father," and we respond, "May the Lord accept the sacrifice at your hands." I offer not only my financial gifts but my body, my blood, my soul, and my life for His good purpose and intentions. I unite all my suffering, the totality of my life, to His suffering as reparation for whom I offer Mass. This is my "sliver of the Cross" as St. Pio said. It is the essence of what we pray in the Morning Offering Prayer.

The Mass has the power to save a whole city from the wrath of God's vengeance. Jesus told St. Faustina He would punish a city in Poland as He did Sodom and Gomorrah. Instead, through her intercession, He said, "My child, unite yourself closely to Me during the Sacrifice and offer My Blood and My wounds to My Father in expiation for the sins of that city. Repeat this without interruption throughout the entire Holy Mass. Do this for seven days."[14] The city was spared.

Masses can free souls from purgatory. Many souls in purgatory came to St. Pio on the way to heaven to thank him for the Masses he said were for them.

* * * * *

Saint Pio, true to his calling as a representative of Christ, participated in the Passion of the Mass both in time and in his flesh. It was the joining of his body with Christ's in the Mass that Saint Pio was able to have great intercessory power with God. He was a true living sacrifice of love that was united to Christ in the sacrifice. In his participation of the Mass this way, he fulfilled the sanctifying of himself and others.

As we spend time with Christ in the Last Supper of the Mass and offer ourselves to the Father in the offertory, we will see graces bestowed upon us—and upon those we offer in our intentions. This is the beginning of "the way of Padre Pio."

As for the Mass, I learned, through the mercy of God, and continue to learn, its importance and eternal value, its necessity to live the Christian life, its power to alter lives, and the need to have the Real Presence of Christ in me. In the Mass, united with Christ, I begin to make reparation for those I pray.

In His Own Words

Padre, does the Lord love the sacrifice?
Yes, because with it He regenerated the world.

How much glory does the Holy Mass give God?
Infinite glory.

What do we gain by hearing the Mass?
The benefits cannot be reckoned [sic]. You will see them in Heaven.[15]

Each holy Mass, heard with devotion, produces in our souls marvelous effects, abundant spiritual and material graces which we ourselves, do not know.[16]

It would be easier for the earth to carry on without the sun than without the Mass.[17]

If people knew the value of the Mass, there would be policemen at the door, to regulate access to the church every time that a Mass is celebrated.[18]

The benefits of the Mass cannot be enumerated. We will know them in Paradise.[19]

Always stay close to the Catholic Church, because it alone can give you true peace, because it alone possesses Jesus in the Blessed Sacrament, who is the true Prince of Peace.[20]

You ask me if it is a useful thing to apply the sacrifice of the Mass for the living. It is extremely useful and holy to apply this sacrifice while one is a pilgrim on this earth, and it will help us to live a holy life, and extinguish the debts contracted with divine justice, and render the most sweet Lord more benevolent towards us.[21]

---

[1] Morcaldi, p. 187.
[2] Vianney, p. 37.
[3] Ibid, p. 37.
[4] Kowalska, p. 45 (#91).
[5] Ibid, p. 644 (#1826).
[6] Ibid, p. 638 (#1804).
[7] Ibid, p. 494 (#1385).
[8] Marison, p. 372.

[9] Ibid, p. 372.
[10] Ibid, p. 373.
[11] Ibid, p. 374.
[12] Ibid, p. 374.
[13] Ratzinger, p. 626.
[14] Michalenko, p. 41 (#39).
[15] Da Cervinara, p. 42–43.
[16] Pio, 2018, p. 119.
[17] Ibid, p. 119.
[18] Capuano, p. 76.
[19] Morcaldi, p. 181.
[20] Pio, 2018, p. 161.
[21] Pio, 1999, p. 95.

Padre Pio's Mass

"Padre, tell me all that you suffer in the Holy Mass."
All that Jesus suffered in His passion, inadequately, I also
suffer, as far as it is possible for a human being.[1]

—St. Pio

Renovations came to the parish one year. Our new pastor, fresh out of ordination, was given the task of securing a new place of worship as one of his past occupations was in construction. He used his experience to locate and put up a large worship tent in the parish's parking lot. Once the tent was up and our plans for the altar were in place, the city ordinance team was called. Of course, according to the city, we were out of compliance. The altar had no handicap access ramp. Now our parish priests were all too healthy and did not need a ramp. So that was the argument. However, the city is the city, and we needed a ramp. A permit was not going to be issued until a ramp was put in. And so it goes.

Well, shortly after the completion of the tent according to city code and the community of worshippers were allowed in, our "construction" priest had his back go out. Oh, the pain and embarrassment of having to do Mass in a wheelchair. Little did he know he would be the one to need a wheelchair ramp! (The planning of God in the little things.)

When the time came to consecrate the Host in the Mass, the priest grabbed the altar in an attempt to stand and hold the Host up. In his attempt, the sciatic nerve sent spasms throughout his body. His face contorted and body twitched from the pain. And so, it was at every Mass; with every Consecration, there was pain. In this, he definitely participated, to a small degree, in the suffering and sacrifice of the Mass.

* * * * *

How would you spend time before Mass knowing you were to *participate* in it? How would you prepare to be scourged, crowned with thorns, carry a cross, and then be nailed *on it* with Jesus? What if God, in His wisdom, allowed you to participate in His Son's Passion by allowing you to experience a bit of the Passion with each consumption of Host and Blood? What if every presiding priest bled with the consecration of bread and wine?

Padre Pio, the Capuchin priest from San Giovanni Rotundo, Italy, at each Mass he presided, was given the grace of experiencing the Passion of our Lord from the Garden of Gethsemane to the scourging on the pillar, the crowning with thorns, the carrying of the cross, to the crucifixion and death. The grace of bearing what Jesus bore, in as much as a human can, is what allowed Padre Pio such great access to the throne of the Father. His ability to intercede for others and move the heart of God came from the desire to know and participate in the Passion of Christ.

Padre Pio's participation in the Passion of the Mass and bearing the wounds of Christ brought the authority to make reparation and intercession for others.

* * * * *

Padre Pio rose every morning at three thirty to prepare for the five-o'clock Mass. Putting on his robes was a painful process. It was done with the assistance of another in his later years. He would prepare for Mass with meditation and prayer, always to include the Rosary. Outside the monastery, in the cold, dark morning, wet or dry, often traveling miles to be present at his Mass, many waited. When the monastery doors opened, the crowd would rush to the front to be as close to Padre Pio as possible. He often needed the help of a fellow brother to walk through the crowd as the wounds on his feet bled.

When the Mass began, there was only silence. Those who attended his Mass were never the same. They spoke of being in Heaven and seeing heavenly things. The Mass could last as long as two and a half hours.

In the Words of Others

Padre Pio Capuano:

> There is no report of any other place in the world where people would be waiting for hours at the locked door of a church, rain or shine, or snow or wind, or cold, to attend a Mass celebrated at four or five in the morning.[2]

Oscar De Liso:

> As Padre Pio goes into ecstasy during the Mass, he becomes a spectacle of agony. His eyes are shut, his face contorted in pain, his lips trembling, his cheeks wet with tears. His ecstasy lasts long, while he relives the Passion of the Cross. For several minutes he leans on the altar and weeps, standing perfectly still in mystical transport. The expression of his face is that of a nomad of the beyond.[3]

Bishop Giuseppe Petralia:

> Padre Pio's Mass was a mission of reparation. In the Mass he lived over again in his body the tragedy of the Passion. Padre Pio was made to suffer the agony of the Gethsemane, the scourging in the praetorium, the crowning with thorns,

the mockery of the crowd, the humiliation of the
unjust sentence, the carrying of the Cross, and
the crucifixion.[4]

Luigi Peroni:

> On the altar, in Padre Pio's flesh, the whole
> Passion is lived again: the agony, scourging,
> thorns, crucifixion, and the piercing of the chest
> with a lance.[5]

Bill Carrigan:

> Carrigan noticed a transformation in Padre
> Pio during the consecration; he seemed to 'take
> on physical sufferings... At the words of the
> consecration, he seemed to have great difficulty
> speaking the words, '*Hoc est entim corpus meum*'
> (This is my body). Carrigan noted that Padre Pio
> shouted the words, hesitating and biting them off
> 'as if the pain were so great he could not grasp it.'
> His facial muscles were twitching and tears were
> rolling down his cheeks. Occasionally, 'he jerked
> his head to one side or the other, as if he were
> suffering blows to the head and neck.' After the
> consecration, it seemed as if Padre Pio's suffering
> had subsided, and he appeared exhausted, lean-
> ing forward as if in deep meditation.[6] (William
> Carrigan, of the Fifteenth Air Force, assigned at
> Christmas 1943 to the American Red Cross field
> office in Foggia.)

Don Pierino Galeone:

> I have seen Padre Pio on the altar taking the
> appearance of Jesus.[7]

Wanda Poltawska:

> The Mass lasted a long time, but the people who filled the church were completely still, transfixed by the Eucharist made real to them by this extraordinary man.[8]

Alberto Del Fante:

> During the Mass Padre Pio reenacts the Passion, becoming a living sacrificial victim.[9]

Padre Marcellino Iasenzaniro:

> One can only say that it was clearly perceivable that (Padre Pio) was in agony and had difficulty celebrating that sacred rite, after stopping for a long time at the consecration formula: "This is My body. This is My Blood." It was the moment in which *he joined in the offering of the divine victim*, the Son of God who gives His life for mankind… He stayed completely still in ecstasy from this meeting with Christ. As he prayed "Lamb of God," he would weep. "People assisted dumbfounded, amazed and moved."[10] (Italics mine)

In His Own Words

> "Padre, what is your Mass?"
> "A sacred fix with the Passion of Jesus. My responsibility is unique in the world" (he says sobbing).

> "Padre, tell me all that you suffer in the Holy Mass."

"All that Jesus has suffered in His Passion, inadequately, I also suffer, as far as is possible for a human being."

"Padre, do you agonize like Jesus in the garden?"
"Surely."

"Does the Angel also come to comfort you as he comforted Jesus?"
"Yes."

"Padre, when you are scourged during the night, are you alone or is there someone with you?
"The Holy Virgin is with me; all Paradise is present."

"Are you then also one entire wound from head to toe?"
"Isn't that the glory of it all? I do not desire to suffer for suffering's sake, no, but for the fruits for which it gives. It gives glory to God and saves my brethren."

"Padre, is it true that during Mass you suffer the torment of the crowning with thorns?"
"And need you doubt it?"

"During all the Mass?"
"And also prior to the Mass and after. The diadem is always present."

"Padre, do you suffer what Jesus suffered on the way to the Cross?"

"I do suffer it, but I'm far from equaling that which the Divine Master suffered."

"Who acts as your Cyrenian and as your Veronica?"
"Jesus Himself."

"Padre, do you take our iniquities upon yourself, in the divine sacrifice?"
"I cannot do otherwise since that is part of the divine sacrifice."

"I have seen you tremble as you went up the steps to the altar. Why? Was it for which you were about to suffer?"
"Not for that which I had to suffer, but for that which I had to offer." (There is nothing which the Padre does not suffer, because he offers himself entirely.)

"Which is the moment during the celebration of the Holy Mass when you suffer most?"
"From the consecration to the Communion."

"During which part of the Mass do you suffer the scourging?"
"From beginning to the end, but more intensely after the consecration."

"Are the stings of the crown of thorns and the wounds of the scourging real during the Mass?"
"What do you mean by this? The effect is the same all right."

"Why do you cry at the offertory?

"It is the moment when the soul is separated from all that which is profane.

"Tell me why you suffer so much at the consecration."
"Because right then a new and admirable destruction and creation takes place."

"Do you suffer the bitterness of the gall?"
"Yes, and very often."

"When at the altar, do you hang on the cross like Jesus on Calvary?"
"And you need ask?"

"Do you suffer the thirst and abandonment of Jesus?"
"Yes."

"When do you suffer the thirst and abandonment of Jesus?"
"After the consecration."

"Up to which moment do you suffer the abandonment and the thirst?"
"Usually up to the Communion."

"You have said you are ashamed to admit you tried, in vain, to find some comfort. Why?"
"Because in comparison to what Jesus had to suffer, our suffering, as the real guilty ones, is a mere nothing."

"Do you also die in the Holy Mass?"
"Mystically in Holy Communion."

"Does the Most Holy Virgin attend your Mass?"

"And do you suppose the Mother to have no interest in the Son?"

"Do the Angels attend your Mass?"
"In multitudes."

"Padre, in what manner should we hear Holy Mass?"

"In the same manner the Most Holy Virgin and… St. John took part in the sacrifice of the Eucharist and the sacrifice of blood of the Cross."[11]

* * * * *

These words are a window into the mystery of Padre Pio's union with Christ in the Mass. In the offering of himself so completely with the Son of God to the Father at the moment of consecration, he completed his mission to sanctify himself and sanctify others. When St. Pio uttered the words, "This is My Body," though they were *Christ's words*, they were also *his*. This offering, and the pain it caused, was both reparation and expiation for those he prayed for.

Therefore, the wounds of the crucifixion (the wounds, the crucifixion, and the stigmata) that Padre Pio had for 58 years had exactly this scope: that of assuming the sins and the scope of expiating them with sufferings.[12] (Dom Perino Galeone)

St. Pio continued to live the Passion of our Lord outside the Mass through the wounds of Christ. He carried the stigmata until his last Mass on September 22, 1968, when they no longer appeared on his body. Though St. Pio had other scars from operations performed, the wounds of the stigmata left no marks.

How powerful the effect on our lives would be, how great the graces received, how great our intercession for others, if we were to participate in the Passion of our Lord as St. Pio did. We can only, at best, offer our sufferings in the Mass as wounds to be united to the suffering of Christ on the Cross. This is "the way of Padre Pio." In the end, in Heaven, we will see just how poor we were at suffering.

---

[1]   da Cervinara, p. 20.
[2]   Capuano, p. 75.
[3]   De Liso, p. 10.
[4]   Ingoldsby, pp.99–100.
[5]   Peroni, pp. 415–416.
[6]   Ruffin, p. 295.
[7]   Galeone, p. 69.
[8]   Gallagher, p.183.
[9]   Ingoldsby, p.194.
[10] Ruffin, p. 332.
[11] da Cervinara, pp. 20–43.
[12] Galeone, "Together With Padre Pio."

Spiritual Children

When the Lord entrusts a soul to me, I place
it on my shoulder and never let it go.[1]

—St. Pio

When Elio Leonardi was a little boy, his
mother often took him to see Padre Pio. She told
Elio that after she put him under the protection
of Padre Pio, he was assisted on numerous occasions. She said that at least five or six times, Elio
had been miraculously protected by Padre Pio
and kept from harm's way. Elio listened to his
mother politely, but was never really convinced
that what she said was true.

One day, when Elio was walking down the
road in San Giovanni Rotondo to catch a bus, a
car hit him from behind. Elio was thrown into
the air from the impact and flew over the top of
the car. Elio saw, upside down, the statue of the
Virgin Mary which was on top of the church.

"'Madonna, I beg You to help me!" Elio
prayed quickly and with great intensity.

Elio was rushed to the Home of the Relief
of Suffering where he had a thorough examination. He knew that he was very lucky to be alive.
After he was released from the hospital, he rushed
over to the monastery and was surprised to see

that all of the monastery doors were open. Padre Pio happened to be praying in the choir loft at the time. Elio burst into tears as he approached Padre Pio. He fell to his knees in front of him and said, "Thank you, Padre Pio! Thank you for saving my life!"

"Don't thank me," Padre Pio replied. "Thank the Madonna. It was She who saved you." Padre Pio smiled at Elio and with an expression of immense love he added, "My son, I can never leave you alone for a minute!"[2]

Recorded in the collected stories *Pray, Hope, and Don't Worry* by Diane Allen, this story happened long ago. But the words Padre Pio uttered are as true today as when he first said them.

* * * * *

True today?

My daughter lives at a state college and works a part-time job. She often arrives late in the evening to the school campus. The parking for her dorm is often filled by the time she arrives which means she must walk a long distance across campus at night. As a concerned Dad, I either call or text her to make sure she has arrived safe.

Recently, I texted her knowing she was going to be late. Her answer warmed my heart. She recanted this story:

> I could not find parking, Dad. So I texted my friends from the dorm's group chat to ask if anyone knew where parking was. One of my guy friends answered. He said he would help find parking and walk back with me.
>
> When I pulled up to the dorm to pick my friend up, there were four of my guy friends! They all piled into my car, and we drove around until we found parking. I am safe in my dorm![3]

Was Saint Pio watching her? In my heart of faith, I know he was. I have consecrated my whole family to both Padre Pio and Mother Mary. Nothing can happen to them unless it is allowed by our Lord, *but not without intercession* from Mother Mary and my spiritual father, Padre Pio.

St. Pio knew his spiritual children before they knew him. His promise to care and watch over them is eternal. His love was paternal with a warning to hit them if they embarrassed him before the Lord. In truth, he was held accountable before God for our actions.

But he was truly a loving father who, if needed, and with permission from God the Father, would take on the physical sufferings of the one for whom he prayed. Here are two of my favorite intercessions: Giovanni Savino and Gemma Di Giorgi. To this day, there is no scientific explanation for their cures.

* * * * *

In 1949, Giovanni Savino, a spiritual child of Padre Pio, was working on the soon to be Casa Sollievo della Sofferenza hospital as a dynamite setter. St. Pio had warned him of an upcoming disaster but had prayed he would not die. Giovanni was to be involved in a dynamite blast that would rip through his face and gouge his eye out.

After the incident, in the hospital, Giovanni sent word to St. Pio. He would rather die than live as a cripple and asked Padre Pio to pray for him. At the Lady of Grace monastery where Padre Pio lived, it was heard of Padre Pio to pray, "Lord, I give you one of my eyes for Giovanni since he is the father of a family."[4]

After ten days in the hospital, the facial bandages were removed. The skin looked as though nothing had happened. There was no trace of injury. The eye that had been completely destroyed was seeing fine, though the socket was empty. The eye that had been damaged, but was intact, could see nothing.

When Giovanni went to see Padre Pio to thank him for the healing, St. Pio said, "Let us thank God you did not die! If only you knew what this cost me!"[5]

* * * * *

In 1947, along with her grandmother, Gemma di Giorgi went to see Padre Pio. One of her relatives was a nun and knew of him. She had suggested they take Gemma to see him for healing after the aunt had a dream where St. Pio made the sign of the cross over Gemma's eyes. Gemma was born without pupils. She was now seven years old.

While riding on a train to see him, she began to see shadows out the window on the landscape. Upon arriving at Our Lady of Grace and speaking to Padre Pio during confession, he made the sign of the cross over Gemma's eyes. Upon her leaving, he said, "Be good and be saintly."[6] Although Gemma had no irises, she saw perfectly well. Today, it is known Gemma suffered from aniridia, a condition where the eye lacks an iris. Through the intercession of Padre Pio, she was given sight. While giving her testimony in the Philippines in 2003, Gemma said, "I see with the eyes of God, not the eyes of my body."[7]

* * * * *

My own journey to St. Pio began in 2016 with a strong interest in St. Mother Teresa. Her love, service, and simplicity captivated me. She spoke of serving others through suffering and the offering of that pain for others. The idea of redemptive suffering led me to St. Faustina and the Divine Mercy. Ultimately, St. Pio revealed himself.

About the same time, I was heading a Confraternity of Christian Doctrine (CCD) class in my home. As a Christmas gift, I ordered Padre Pio rosaries for the group. Early the next year, I asked Padre Pio to accept me as a spiritual child and asked for confirmation he had accepted me. A few weeks later, I received a package with twelve Padre Pio rosaries in it. Neither I, nor anyone in my family, ordered rosaries. I contacted the company that sent them. It was the same company I had ordered the first twelve Padre Pio rosaries. They had no record of sending them. I offered to pay for them if they sent a bill. I took this as a *yes* from Padre Pio.

Most of the twelve rosaries went to the founding members of the Padre Pio prayer group started at my parish. From there, the story grows, but that is another book.

Claiming Padre Pio's assistance comes with conditions. The spiritual children of Padre Pio know that he asks them to do the following:

1. Live intensely on God's grace and make use of the sacraments of Eucharist and reconciliation often.
2. Live one's faith in words and actions, in a true Christian life.
3. Love Jesus Christ crucified, the Most Blessed Sacrament, our Blessed Mother, the Holy Father, and the Roman Catholic Church.
4. Be proactive and animated by a sincere spirit of charity toward all.

Today, these are the core values of the Padre Pio prayer groups. Through them, we can ask for his intercession and continue his mission to save souls, empty purgatory, and fulfill His love in us by living a life of love, reparation, and sacrifice. We must learn to sanctify ourselves and sanctify others, to rejoice in our sufferings for the sake of those we pray for and fill up what is lacking in the afflictions of Christ (Colossians 1:24).

It was the love for his children that Father Pio offered himself in their place. Through his obedience and trust, God the Father answered his prayers of sacrifice. Can we not do the same? It is "the way of Padre Pio."

In His Own Words

Always keep close to God. In Him I am with you, more than you can know.[8]

I know my spiritual children and they will know me. I knew you when you were four years old, and I knew you when you were fifteen years old. God entrusted you to me on the day you were born.[9]

I can forget myself, but I cannot forget my Children. I tell you that when the Lord calls me, I will stay at the door of Paradise and will tell Him, "Lord, I will not enter before I see that all my Children have entered."[10]

After I die, I will be closer to you than I am now. I will watch over you better, because I won't be suffering there.[11]

I love my spiritual children as much as my own soul and even more.[12]

When I have lifted a soul, I don't let it fall down again.[13]

When a soul approaches me, I take it. When I have taken a soul, I never let it go.[14]

I belong entirely to everyone. Everyone can say: Padre Pio is mine.[15]

After my death I will do more. My real mission will begin after my death.[16]

---

[1]   Alberto, p. 161.
[2]   Allen, 2011, pp. 377–378.
[3]   Moncayo, J. September 2019.
[4]   Allen, 2012, pp. 66–67.
[5]   Ibid. p. 68.
[6]   Ibid. p. 271.
[7]   Ruffin, p. 377.
[8]   Allen, 2012, p. 185.
[9]   Ibid, p. 285–286.
[10]   Morcaldi, p. 81.
[11]   Iasenzaniro, p. 651.
[12]   Pio, 2010, p. 549.

[13] Winowska, p. 47.
[14] D'Apolito, p. 149.
[15] Pio, 2018, p. 174.
[16] Allen, 2012, p. 1.

St. Pio's Madonna

She comes to me whenever I need Her.[1]

—St. Pio

Most people who have been Catholics since childhood have a story about Mother Mary. Having been brought up to honor her in church and around the house, I learned her presence. But not until I entered adulthood did I come to love her as my Mother.

Well, *my story* does not part any Red Seas or cause me to walk on water, but it helps to show her presence in my family.

* * * * *

Having walked our two beagles earlier, I decided the stubborn one needed more practice. I told the wife I was taking him around one more time to practice commands. Having come around one house we had passed earlier, two very small dogs charged out of a slightly open front door and went right at my beagle who was on a tight leash. Aiming for the underside of my dog, testicles to be exact, they bit into him. As I said earlier, he was on a tight leash, so he really wasn't able to defend himself, especially as I was pulling him away from the two rat-like fiends. As they bit into his testicles, he howled, then bit into my hand that somehow in the melee got caught in his mouth. By this time, the owners, who were watching from the side-walk, picked up the two rats and took them inside. My beagle was bleeding. I was bleeding. So we didn't wait around for the owners to come back out. Later, when I went back to ask him to pay for the vet bills, he said he tried to find me by following the blood on the sidewalk until it disappeared.

In shock, I had picked up my beagle and walked back to my house. I immediately began to pray the Rosary, asking for Mother Mary's help. When we got home, I placed my beagle into the garage tub and began rinsing him. I got my wife to come out who started with a million questions. Not two minutes later, my father and mother-in-law drove up. Of course, they were confused and began to tell the story of how they just *had* to return a sock that belonged to us. *One sock*, and they showed up. My wife and I were trying to figure out how to get both myself and the dog to the hospital with two kids under the age of six. Mother Mary, I know, moved the hearts of my in-laws to return the sock just when they did. My in-laws spent most of the night with my girls while my wife drove our beagle to the animal hospital and I to the emergency room. We both had shots, my beagle stitches. I cannot imagine having the two girls with us that night and going through all the trauma.

Mother Mary covered us with Her mantle. *She came to me when I needed Her.*

* * * * *

The relationship between St. Pio and Mother Mary was lifelong. As a child, Francesco Forgione (Padre Pio), often conversed with Jesus and Mary. Such apparitions were given to Pio to prepare him for the spiritual world he would live in.

As an adult, he would say of Her,

> I feel like a sailing ship, pushed by our heavenly Mother's breath. Even if I am lost on the high seas, I'm not worried. I can't say where I start, nor where my various works will end, but I never feel uncertain because I am spiritually directed by Her. She accompanies me in the confessional, to let me aid my brothers and sisters, and She shows me, already covered by the veil

of Her pity, the numberless souls waiting for an absolution which will destroy all evils and be the creator of all good.[2]

She was always by his side and would often refer to her as the Madonna. Those who served with Padre Pio knew of his devotion to Her. Always curious about his life, they would ask short questions, hoping for a glimpse into the spiritual. Bernard Ruffin, in his biography of Padre Pio, records such a conversation.

> Padre Tarcisio Zullo da Cervinara and Padre Mariano da Magliano Santa Croce were in Padre Pio's room. They took the courage and asked him: "Father, is the Madonna *at this moment* in this room?" Padre Pio's answer: "Wrong formulation. You should have asked, 'Did the Madonna ever leave this room?'"[3]

Often, in his demonic attacks, Mother Mary was by his side. She would allow the attacks (as we must all face temptation and battle the evil that God allows). But in her love for Padre Pio, she tempered the attacks by intervening at key moments. In one such attack, a demon threw St. Pio to the floor. When other priests heard his cries and commotion, they entered his room. They found him on the floor bruised, bleeding, and his head on a pillow. At the moment of impact, the Blessed Mother had placed a pillow under his head to soften the blow.

She aided him in the task of absolution in the confessional where he was able to recite his many rosaries. On several occasions, Padre Pio confided to his confreres that the Blessed Virgin remained beside him while he heard confessions. She was his help in his suffering and need. Padre Marcellino remarked, "Padre Pio solves everything with the help of our Lady, or by letting her solve it."[4]

She was with him in the Mass. To Enzo Bertani, he said, "Every morning the Virgin Mary is at the altar, together with Jesus, or the Seraphic Father Saint Francis."[5]

She was with him when no one else could be. Twice in his life, Padre Pio was ordered to celebrate Mass by himself—once in May 1923, and again from June 1931 to July 1933. The second time, Padre Pio was stripped of his priestly faculties, except the faculty to celebrate the Holy Mass, which could only occur in private. Years later, Padre Pio told Padre Eusebio, "I was never alone. Our Lady always kept me company during Mass."[6]

Padre Pio spoke lovingly of Her. When asked by a woman the quickest way to Heaven, he replied,

> "The shortcut…is the Virgin. The Holy Virgin…is the perfect example of God's mercy on earth. She acts as His double… She is the one who brings us a ray of God's immensity and of divine powers… I am spiritually directed by Her… She accompanies me in the confessional, to let me aid my brothers and sisters.[7]

He was known for advocating her Rosary. It was his weapon to fight Hell as he often said, "This is my weapon. With this, I win the battle."[8] He was never without a Rosary in his hand, and had one sewn into his robe to pray with while doing other things. He was often seen fingering his Rosary beads he had sown into his cloak.

Padre Fernando da Riese reported:

> The Rosary was Padre Pio's favored prayer. He prayed it many times a day, decade after decade. He always had a rosary wrapped around his hand or his arm, as though it was a jewel or a shield. He had other rosaries under the pillow and on the nightstand. He called the Rosary his "weapon." He had made a resolution years earlier to say no less than five complete rosaries every day.[9]

On February 6, 1954, at 9:00 p.m., when Father Carmelo asked how many Rosaries Padre Pio had prayed, he replied, "I still have two Rosaries to pray today. I said only thirty-four so far. Then I will go to bed."[10]

When asked by another priest how many rosaries Padre Pio had said that day, he replied, "Today I said thirty-two or thirty-three Rosaries. Maybe one or two more." To Padre Mariano Paladino da Magliano Santa Croce, he said, "About thirty. Maybe some more but not less." Padre Mariano asked, "How do you do it?" He replied, "What is the night for?" To Don Pierino Galeone, he said, "Between fifteen and twenty."[11]

Padre Alessio Parente, one of Padre Pio's personal assistants, wrote,

> I was at Padre Pio's side for six years, and in all that time I never saw him without a Rosary in his hands, night and day. Our lady never refused him anything through the Rosary… The Rosary was Padre Pio's constant link with our Mother.[12]

Why was the Rosary so important to Padre Pio? "The Rosary is the prayer of those who triumph over everything and everyone. It was Our Lady who taught us this prayer, just as it was Jesus who taught us the Our Father."[13]

The Madonna was with him to the end. A few minutes before dying, sitting in his armchair in his room of fifty-two years, clutching his rosary, Padre Pio said, "I see two mothers."[14] His own mother had died many years before. In the last moments of his life, Padre Pio was seeing both the Virgin Mary and his birth mother, Peppa, together. His very last words were "Jesus. Mary."[15]

To separate the Madonna from Padre Pio was to separate his soul from God. The two were inseparable. She was a mother to him when his birth mother could not be. In the end, they both came for him, together.

* * * * *

For us, as spiritual children of Padre Pio, we must nurture our own relationship with the Mother of God. We cannot know Padre Pio without knowing his Madonna. To her has been given all the graces of Heaven to disperse as she sees fit, according to the Father's will.

May we strive to know the Madonna as Padre Pio did so that she may *assist us* in our Dark Night.

In His Own Words

I don't have to go to Lourdes. I go there every night.[16]

There are people so foolish that they think they can go through life without the help of the Madonna.[17]

Oh Mary, sweet Mother of priests, mediatrix and administratrix of all graces, from the bottom of my heart I beg and implore you to thank Jesus, the fruit of thy womb, today, tomorrow and forever.[18]

Do Purgatory here accepting from the Hand of the Lord all that He sends, offering it to Him united with the merits and sufferings of the Madonna.[19]

Let us make her loved and let's pray the Rosary that she taught us.[20]

---

[1] Ingoldsby, p. 136.
[2] Ruffin, p. 177.
[3] Ingoldsby, p. 136.
[4] Iasenzaniro, p.664.
[5] Ibid, p. 665.

6   Ibid, p. 668.
7   Ruffin, p. 177.
8   Napolitano, p. 217.
9   da Riese, p. 486.
10 Napolitano, pp. 222–223.
11 Galeone, p. 44.
12 Allen, 2012, p. 36.
13 Ibid, p. 34.
14 Ruffin, p. 450.
15 Ibid, p. 450.
16 Schug, p. 59.
17 Allen, 2012, p. 34.
18 Pio, 2018, p. 86.
19 Ruffin, p. 343.
20 Ibid, p. 349.

Spring Cleaning (Confession)

To rouse certain souls, you need cannonballs. Treating them
with gentleness is a waste of time. They need to feel God's
anger when the strength of His mercy is not enough[1]

—Padre Pio

Padre Pio was notorious for turning away confessors whom he
believed had no real remorse for their sins. By refusing absolution
to each unrepentant confessor, St. Pio was offering a "severe mercy."
It was a way of guiding them toward the redemptive life of penance
and reparation.

In his book about the life, death, and conversion of his wife,
Sheldon Vanauken (1914–1996) writes how the death of his wife
brought about his conversion to Catholicism. After her conversion,
she offered her life to God for the conversion of her husband. C. S.
Lewis, a dear friend of Vanauken, after he reached out to his friend
for advice, called this a "severe mercy." He defines this as "a mercy
as severe as death, a severity as merciful as love."[2] God was being
merciful by granting the grace of Vanauken's conversion, but acting
severely by allowing the death of his wife to bring God's grace into
his life. The offering of one life for another is the ultimate act of
redemptive suffering, the last act of love and sacrifice.

How is a sacrifice measured? It is measured by the *severity* of
what is sacrificed and the *willingness* to give it. In our lives, it is measured by our willingness to suffer for those we love and pray for.
When we practice it, we become like the Savior. In her diary, St.
Faustina Kowalska wrote, "The greater the suffering, the purer the

love."[3] It is not in the degree of suffering that we resemble our Lord, but in the love that motivates and offers it.

The offering of His Son by the Father—to leave the eternal bliss of Heaven, and take on the life of a human—was the ultimate severe mercy. In the end, it was the most extreme suffering God could place on any human for the most redemption possible—*for all sins ever committed by the entire human race for all time*. It is suffering, by a man, only God could do. It is His love, measured by the willingness to take on the world's debt, for all time, for every human ever existed, and pay its price. It is our Lord's severe mercy for us.

How is this love and sacrifice achieved in us so we may offer severe mercies for others? And possibly, in the smallest way, live the life of penance and reparation?

* * * * *

C. S. Lewis, the great protestant friend of J. R. R. Tolkien, likens the recreation of God's life in us to building a house. It begins to answer what we expect of God in us and what He remakes us into so he can achieve what He expects in us.

> Imagine yourself as a living house. God comes in to rebuild that house. At first, perhaps, you can understand what He is doing. He is getting the drains right and stopping the leaks in the roof and so on: you knew that those jobs needed doing and so you are not surprised. But presently He starts knocking the house about in a way that hurts abominably and does not seem to make sense. What on earth is He up to? The explanation is that He is building quite a different house from the one you thought of—throwing out a new wing here, putting on an extra floor there, running up towers, making courtyards. You thought you were going to be made into a

decent little cottage, but He is building a palace. He intends to come and live in it Himself.[4]

Before the Lord can use us in the lives of others, He must build Himself a place to live, a home where His will is paramount. As He builds, we must remove the sin that keeps Him out. The rebuilding of our soul begins with the removal of sin. It begins with confession.

* * * * *

Padre Pio offered a severe mercy to unrepentant souls by not giving them absolution for the purpose of awakening in them a need for God in their lives. Yet even as they walked away from the confessional, Padre Pio sought reparation for them. A man who St. Pio had dismissed three times without absolution explained, "Now, I understand the gravity of my failings. Up to then no one had really shaken me, so that I easily justified my errors to myself."[5]

Why was Padre Pio so adamant about being honest with God in the confessional? Why did he place so much importance on the purity and necessity of the sacrament of reconciliation enough to withhold it from those who had little or no remorse? Why did he spend most of his ministry in the confessional, up to eighteen hours a day? Before love and sacrifice, there must be remorse and confession. Before we can offer ourselves, we must be pure of soul. We must confess our sins. This is how love and sacrifice begin in us.

His advice to those who sought mercy and restoration with the Father?

> What else can I say to you? May the grace and peace of the Holy Spirit always be at the center of your heart. Place your heart in the open side of the Savior and unite it with the King of our hearts who is within it as on a royal throne, in order that he might receive homage and obedience from all other hearts.[6]

Can the "grace and peace of the Holy Spirit always be at the center of your heart…within it as on a royal throne" when it is filled with sin? If God is holy, and nothing impure can enter heaven, how can a holy God enter an impure heart? How then shall we confess so that the Holy Spirit can be at the center of our heart? St. Pio tells us,

> When you fall, do not stay there prostrated in the body and spirit. Humble yourself greatly but without being discouraged. Lower yourself without degrading yourself. Wash your imperfections and falls with sincere tears of contrition, without lacking trust in divine goodness, which will always be greater than your ingratitude. Propose to make amends without being presumptuous, but your strength must be in God alone. Finally, confess sincerely that if God were not your breast-plate and shield, you would be imprudently pierced with every kind of sin.[7]

St. Pio often said it was a humble and a contrite heart that won over God.

Jesus told St. Faustina in the book, *The Life of Faustina Kowalska,*

> Every time you go to confession, immerse yourself entirely in My mercy, with great trust, so that I may pour the bounty of My grace upon your soul. When you approach the confessional, know this, that I Myself am waiting there for you. I am only hidden by the priest, but I Myself act in your soul. Here the misery of the soul meets the God of mercy. Tell the souls that from this fount of mercy souls draw graces solely with the vessel of trust. If their trust is great, there is no limit to My generosity. The torrents of grace inundate humble souls. The proud remain always in poverty and misery.[8]

The Sacrament of Reconciliation is His opportunity to wash away our sin, clean our soul, and create in us a new heart, one that reflects His. In Reconciliation, Padre Pio helped others find sanctification. With Jesus on the throne of our heart and the Holy Spirit our guide, we are open to His leading with the power to sacrifice for others empowered by the love of God the Father. In short, confession offers the cleansing of the soul whereby we receive His love and graces needed to sacrifice. We become closer to God in spirit; His presence in us is greater. His love is purer and our willingness to sacrifice for others greater. We become like Him as He builds a mansion where He can live.

In her diary, Jesus said to St. Faustina of her soul,

> You must be destroyed in that secret depth where the human eye has never penetrated; then will I find you a pleasing sacrifice, a holocaust full of sweetness and fragrancy. And great will be your power for whomever you intercede.[9]

* * * * *

Lent is a perfect time to renew our relationship with Christ through Confession and Communion, and obtain graces for those we love. It is a time to cleanse ourselves of what hinders His love in us; it is our "forty days" in the desert "praying and fasting" with Christ and offering our sufferings and sacrifices, our "severe mercies" to Him, as reparation for ourselves and others. In the cleansing of our souls, Christ may bestow upon us and those we pray for, the graces needed to find redemption, healing, and peace. In doing so, we may avoid the severe mercies brought upon us through a hardened and unrepentant heart.

St. Faustina shares in her diary how important confession and Communion are to the soul who seeks Him in this process of living the redemptive life.

On confession, Jesus wanted her to know how important her confessor was. Once, when she had finished a novena to the Holy Spirit for the intentions of her confessor, the Lord said to her:

> I made him known to you even before
> your superiors had sent you here. As you will act
> toward your confessor, so I will act toward you. If
> you conceal something from him, even though it
> be the least of My graces, I too, will hide Myself
> from you and you will remain alone.[10]

It is important for us to visit our confessor, *who is Jesus*! "When you approach the confessional, know this, that I Myself am waiting there for you. I am only hidden by the priest, but I Myself act in your soul."[11]

On Communion, "But I want to tell you that eternal life must begin already here on earth through Holy Communion. Each Holy Communion makes you more capable of communing with God throughout eternity."[12] "Now you shall consider My love in the Blessed Sacrament. Here, I am entirely yours, soul, body and divinity, as your Bridegroom."[13]

In these two sacraments are the graces needed to live the redemptive life—to sanctify us through the cleansing of the soul in confession, and receiving the Holy Eucharist—the Real Presence of God. They are the brick and mortar for the new building, the means He recreates Himself in us.

* * * * *

We must learn to pray this: *Father, remove from me anything that is not of You.* In this way, confessing our sins comes easier, even a necessity to building a holier home for Him. His light in us becomes brighter while overcoming our darkness. Every act begins with sanctification and with it, eternal value.

Every Lent, as Vanauken's wife did, we can offer ourselves to God for others, freely giving, with no sin as hinderance. Our suffering will open His mercy on those we pray for, and sanctify us along the way. The severity of our sacrifice for others will equal the mercy given to us. As Jesus said to St. Faustina, "I want to see you as a *living sacrifice of love*, which only then carries weight before Me…and great will be your power for whomever you intercede."[14]

We can begin the spring cleaning of our soul through confession by walking through the rooms of our soul, measure the dust of sin gathered, and prepare for the hosting of our King in the Holy Eucharist. In the process, great will be our power for those we intercede. The *purer* the soul through confession, the greater the intercession. James tells us, "The fervent prayer of a righteous person is very powerful" (James 5:16). It is the way of Jesus; it is "the way of Padre Pio."

In His Own Words

On seeking God:

To put on Jesus, we die to ourselves.[15]

On spiritual growth: weekly confession, daily Mass/Communion, spiritual reading, meditation, and examination of conscience.[16]
On confession:

A room needs to be dusted once a week, even if nobody is there.[17]

On Communion:

Unless you are positive you are in mortal sin, you ought to take Communion every day.[18]

On spiritual reading:

If the reading of holy books has the power to convict worldly men into spiritual persons, how very powerful such reading must be in leading spiritual men and women to greater perfection.[19]

On meditation:

> Meditation is the key to progress in the knowledge of self as well as the knowledge of God, and through it we achieve the goal of the spiritual life, which is the transformation of the soul in Christ.[20]

> Try to put yourself in the presence of God and thus understand that, with all the celestial court, He is there within your soul. Then begin your prayer and meditation.[21]

> Recommend yourself to the intercession of the Most Holy Virgin as well as to all the heavenly court, so that they may help you meditate well and keep every distraction and temptation away from you.[22]

> Make it your purpose to amend yourself with regard to that defect which most hinders your union with God and which causes many other defects and sins. Then ask God for all those graces and for all those helps of which you feel the need. Recommend all people to the Lord..., After you have done all this, offer your meditation and your prayer, along with yourself and those closest to your heart. Offer them all to God, along with the merits of Jesus."[23]

On examination of conscience, Padre Pio recommended the morning "to prepare for battle" and the evening "to purify your soul from every earthly affection."[24]

---

[1] Ruffin, p. 340.
[2] Vanauken, p. 211.
[3] Kowalska, p. 29 (#57).
[4] Lewis, p. 205.
[5] Ruffin, p. 340.
[6] Pio, 2018, p. 106.
[7] Ibid, p. 108.
[8] Kowalska, p. 569 (#1602).
[9] Ibid, p. 627 (#1767).
[10] Ibid, p. 130 (#269).
[11] Ibid, p. 569 (#1602).
[12] Ibid, p.640 (#1811).
[13] Ibid, p. 628 (#1770).
[14] Ibid, p. 627 (#1767).
[15] Pio, 2018, p. 100.
[16] Ruffin, p. 170.
[17] Ibid, p. 170.
[18] Ibid, p. 170.
[19] Ibid, p. 170.
[20] Ibid, p. 170.
[21] Ibid, p. 170–171.
[22] Ibid, p. 171.
[23] Ibid, p. 171.
[24] Ibid, p. 171.

Facing the Giant (Spiritual Warfare)

Every spiritual child of Padre Pio has a favorite story of him. Mine
is the formidable warrior. Francesco Forgione, at the age of fifteen,
received a vision in which he saw himself in a huge field. On opposite
sides of the field were two groups of beings. "On one side he saw men
of the most beautiful countenance, clad in snow-white garments. On
the other…he saw men of hideous aspect, dressed in black raiment
like so many dark shadows."[2] At his side was a "majestic man of rare
beauty, resplendent as the sun."[3]

From amidst the dark shadows on the field emerged a man so
hideous and tall it seemed his head touched the sky. The majestic
man told Francesco he must battle this tall man, a formidable warrior. Francesco felt his life was over. About to fall, the majestic man
supported him with one arm until Francesco recovered and begged
the man to spare him from the fight. The man told him the creature
was so strong that the strength of all men combined would not be
enough to defeat him. But if Francesco entered the battle with confidence and trusted this man of rare beauty, he would never leave his
side and would help him defeat the creature. In the end, Francesco
would receive a crown of wondrous beauty.

The battle was ferocious. In the end, with the help of the majestic man, Francesco defeated the creature, and it fled. With the defeat of the creature, all the dark shadows fled, cursing and shrieking. The snow-clad men applauded and praised the majestic man. True to His word, "a crown of rarest beauty…was placed on his head."[4]

Thus, the vision ended. Francesco understood the majestic man was Christ and the tall creature was Satan. He knew Christ was asking him to battle Satan and his kingdom the rest of his life. But the battle would always be won if he trusted Him and entered the battle with confidence.

Francisco Forgione, Padre Pio, continued to battle Satan into his elder years. Padre Alessio, his attendant when Padre Pio was the age of sixty-six, recalled, "He was afraid of devils… One night he called me so many times that I got mad. 'Why don't you let me sleep at least a half-hour?' He said, 'Stay with me! The devils won't leave me alone for one minute!'"[5]

These battles are both physical and spiritual. They are allowed and used by God to *purify* and *sanctify* us. The chief exorcist of the Vatican, Gabriel Amorth, who confessed to St. Pio for twenty-six years, writes,

> The Lord has fixed a trial for everyone. The angels themselves were subjected to this test… Man is also subjected to the test of fidelity to God's laws. This happens…during a time of suffering… Offering oneself to the will of God in suffering is the only path one can take. We are given the opportunity to accept it through the trials of life.[6]

Saint Pio tells us where and why these battles must take place.

> The field of battle between God and Satan is the human soul. This is where it takes place every moment of our lives. The soul must give free access to our Lord and be completely forti-

fied by Him with every kind of weapon; His light must illuminate it (the soul) to fight the darkness of error; he (the soul) must put on Jesus Christ, His truth and justice, the shield of faith, the word of God to overcome such powerful enemies. To put on Jesus Christ, we must die to ourselves.[7]

* * * * *

How are we then to live fighting this dragon the rest of our lives? Jesus told Saint Catherine of Siena,

> I have appointed the devil to tempt and to trouble My creatures in this life. I have done this, not so that My creatures will be overcome, but so that they may overcome… My love permits these temptations, for the devil is weak. He cannot do nothing by himself unless I allow it. So I let him tempt you because I love you, not because I hate you. I want you to conquer, not to be conquered, and to come to a perfect knowledge of yourself and Me.[8]

My response when tempted or battling against a suffering I cannot stand against? Padre Pio tells me,

> Don't make an effort to overcome your temptations, because these efforts would strengthen them. Do not dwell on them. Call Jesus in your imagination, and kissing His side say, "This is my hope. I will hold You tightly, Jesus, and will not let You go until You have placed me in a safe place."[9]

We must realize this is a battle decreed by God for all mankind, subject even to the angels. It is for the removal of sin and the recreation of our soul into His image. With each temptation crushed, each trial won, there is an infusion of God into our lives until we are completely recreated into His image, fully God and fully man. The battle is not only against evil, but with ourselves. The *no* to our nature is a *yes* to His. Our Lord will purify us here, or in purgatory. Nothing impure can enter Heaven.

When I suffer, I offer it as reparation for those whom I pray for. By placing my pain in His hands, I remove it out of reach for Satan to use against me. In His Hands, it becomes power to work in the lives for those whom I pray. As I often say, never waste a good suffering.

The battle is ongoing. It will never end. But it is already won. Our Lady has already crushed the serpent's head; at Fatima, she said, "In the end My Immaculate Heart will triumph." [10]

With St. Pio, we can say the words of Christ, "Enter the battle with confidence. Go forth with courage. I shall be with you." [11]

> St. Pio,
> Pray in me
> St. Pio,
> Pray with me
> St. Pio,
> Pray for me
> St. Pio,
> Pray through me
> To the Father

In His Own Words

Doesn't the Holy Spirit tell us that when the soul approaches God it must prepare itself for temptations? Courage, therefore… Fight valiantly and you will receive the prize of strong souls." [12]

"I know the Lord permits the devil to make these assaults, because His mercy renders you dear to Him, and he wants you to be similar to

Him in the anguish of the desert, the garden and on the Cross.[13]

Say, kissing His side a number of times: "This is my hope; I will hold You tightly, Jesus, until You have placed me in a safe place."[14]

They are the trials of those souls whom God wants to put to the test when He sees them strong enough to sustain the battle, weaving with their own hands, the crown of glory.[15]

Be firmly convinced that the more the assaults of the enemy increase, the closer God is to the soul.[16]

Rest assured that the more a soul is pleasing to God, the more it must be tried. Therefore, courage, and go forward always.[17]

The trials to which the Lord subjects you and will subject you are all signs of divine love and jewels for the soul. Winter will pass and the never-ending spring will come, all the more rich in beauty as violent were the storms.[18]

May it (grace of the Holy Spirit) give you strength to endure the fight and trial to which Jesus is subjecting you for your own sanctification, and the edification of many others.[19]

---

[1] Pio, 1999, p. 18.
[2] Ruffin, p. 38.
[3] Ibid, p. 38.
[4] Ibid, p. 39.
[5] Ibid, p. 444.

6 Amorth, pp. 12–14.
7 Pio, 2018, pp. 99–100.
8 Thigpen, p. 100.
9 Pio, 2018, p. 65.
10 McGlynn, p. 77.
11 Ruffin, pp. 38–39.
12 Pio, 2018, p. 61.
13 Ibid, pp. 62–63.
14 Ibid, p. 65.
15 Ibid, p. 66.
16 Ibid, p. 69.
17 Ibid, p. 70.
18 Ibid, p. 80.
19 Pio, 1999, p. 149.

Dark Night (Alone with God)

For a long time, my soul has found itself immersed day and
night in the deep night of the spirit. My spiritual darkness lasts
for long hours, for days on end, and often for entire weeks.[1]
—Padre Pio

I hesitated as I stood with my Bible over the trash can. It wasn't good
to me anymore. God wasn't listening, and I had just wrecked the side
of my car driving into the garage. That had been the last straw. What
good was there to believe in a God that wasn't doing anything in my
life?

Living with my brothers at their bachelor beach house since the
beginning of summer was depressing enough. At that time in my life,
I could not afford rent anywhere else. They had an extra room and
offered it to me. It was where my son came to visit me on the week-
ends. It was not the best environment with so many beach parties,
but he and I could spend time together on the beach.

The wreck was icing on the cake. I was ready to toss my Bible
into the trash but couldn't do it. As I stood there, I thought of life
without Him. What would be the hope? Even if He was a terrible
God, He was still God. If I did not do things His way, as painful as
they were, I might be lost forever. I stopped in the hope He loved me,
had a plan for me, and that if I held on a little longer, things would
change.

I have heard the saying "God removes the fences we sit on to
make us choose which side we are on with Him." Like David in the
desert, Joseph in the Egyptian prison, Job in his decimation: though

He slay me, yet will I trust Him. Every relationship has a time when the choice is made to continue in it or not. That day was my day to choose. In these dark times, God is nowhere to be found. No prayer is enough.

It's a time when we bargain with God, "If it is not Your will, take it away. What sacrifice can I offer?" In the dark times, it tests our faith. "Why bother? Nothing I do makes a difference! There is no sacrifice acceptable to you. You don't care." In the worst of times, "I won't pray anymore. I won't go to church anymore."

There is emptiness inside. It is our Dark Night—dark because we cannot see or feel anything good, night because it is in the dark we feel alone. It is the name for our purification.

Our comfort in this madness? We are not alone. The great saints, the Spiritual Giants of old, are our company: St. John of the Cross, St. Teresa of Avila, St. Mother Teresa of Calcutta, St. Faustina Kowalska, and, of course, St. Padre Pio of Pietrelcina. The dark night is the way of our Lord. It is "the way of Padre Pio." It is the path we all must take to the Divine. Some walk the path longer, some slower; others never leave it and are consumed by it. Its destination is left to God and the traveler.

* * * * *

It is known by many names: *dark night of the soul, game of love, purgation of the senses* and *infused contemplation*. Protestants call it time in the desert. It teaches submission, obedience, and faith. It infuses God into our soul, removing the old and placing in the new. How we think of Him, how we talk to Him, how we value Him is replaced with His thoughts, His words, His way of loving us. Our words, our thoughts, our feelings are left to the wayside. God begins to move us beyond our world and into His. It is the call in the darkness to come find Him, to let go of everything we value and trust Him. It is a necessary night on the path of redemptive suffering.

Padre Benedetto, Padre Pio's early superior, gave this explanation to Padre Pio when the saint was experiencing his dark night. The dark night is given by God "to extinguish human understanding so that divine understanding can take place, and you, having been stripped of the...usual way of using your mental faculties, might be able to rise to that supernatural and heavenly purification."[2]

The outcome of this night is without word, without thought and emotion. What remains is you and God. You are empty, and He fills you with His presence. To do this, He must remove *all that is you* to allow *all that is Him*—in you. We take off our spectacles and put on His. We learn to speak in His language.

A Closer Look at Saints and Their Dark Night

St. Mother Teresa of Calcutta

St. Mother Teresa of Calcutta (1910–1997) answered the call from Jesus to go into the slums of Calcutta, to "Come be My Light." Jesus said to her,

> I cannot go alone. They don't know me. So, they don't want me. You come—go amongst them, carry Me with you into them. How I long to enter their holes—their dark unhappy homes. Come be their victim. In your immolation—in your love for Me, they will see Me, know Me, want Me.[3]

In her mission to be Jesus, she learned the plight of the slums, to live in darkness, and "how terrible it is to be without God."[4]

In their dark, unhappy homes, they had no sense of God and lived a life without God. In time, she embraced their darkness, won their love, and brought them Jesus. But in doing so, she took onto herself, their darkness.

> The condition of the poor on Calcutta's streets, rejected by all and abandoned to their pain, was, she claimed, "the true picture of my own spiritual life." She had reached the point of

complete identification with her "people," with their misery, loneliness, and rejection.[5]

She, as did Jesus, took on the nature and state of being of those she sought to redeem. By taking on the darkness of those she prayed for, uniting it to the Sacrifice of the Cross, Jesus bestowed upon them the grace of sight and removed their darkness. As they began to live in His light, she began to live in their darkness, *without the sense of His presence.* She had taken on their spiritual plight as Jesus did on the Cross.

Mother Teresa had made a promise to Jesus never to deny Him anything. In her darkness, without the sense of His presence, she continued, by faith and love for Him, not to deny Him anything. In this, she said, "If my darkness is light to some soul—even if it be nothing to nobody—I am perfectly happy—to be God's flower of the field."[6]

This identification with those she helped left her soul empty. She could no longer find Jesus. This was to be her dark night.

> You see, Father, the contradiction in my life.
> I long for God—I want to love Him—to love
> Him very much—to live only for love of Him—
> to love only—and yet there is but pain—longing
> and no love.[7]

In her love for the Savior, she obeyed and prayed, "Jesus, I accept whatever You give—and I give whatever you take."[8] In her most difficult moments, when she did not want to accept what God desired, she prayed, "Deliberately, I took the rosary and very slowly without even meditating or thinking, I said it slowly and calmly."[9]

In taking on the suffering of those she prayed for, she made herself a living sacrifice of love, which, before God, carried much power to intercede. It was her participation in the redemptive work of the Cross. It completed what was lacking in the afflictions of Christ for the church (Colossians 1:24). In her willingness to live within her darkness, refusing to allow her inner suffering to be an excuse not to love and saturate the thirst of Jesus for souls, she kept the promise she made never to deny Him anything.

In Her Own Words

No prayer—no love, no faith—nothing, but continual pain of longing for God.[10]

Pray for me, for the life within me is harder to live. To be in love and yet not to love, to live by faith and yet not to believe. To spend myself and yet be in total darkness. Pray for me.[11]

For only by being one with them we can redeem them, that is, by bringing God into their lives and bringing them to God.[12]

I have come to love the Darkness, for I believe now that it is a part of a very, very small part of Jesus' Darkness and pain on earth.[13]

Smile at the hand that strikes you. Kiss the Hand that is nailing you to the cross.[14]

If I ever become a saint, I will surely be one of "darkness." I will continually be absent from Heaven to light the light of those in darkness on earth.[15]

* * * * *

C.S. Lewis, in his book *The World's Last Night*, asks the question, "Does God then forsake just those who serve Him best? Well, He who served Him best of all said, near His tortured death, 'Why hast thou forsaken me?'"[16] The assumption from Lewis is that we get what we need, when we need it, to do what we need to do. Anymore would tip the heavenly balance in the celestial battle. "If we were stronger, we might be less tenderly trusted. If we were braver, we might be sent, with far less help, to defend far more desperate outposts in the great battle."[17]

From the beginning of creation, a war against sin has raged. The angels were tested, and some were found wanting. God must purify those He seeks to redeem, for nothing unclean can enter Heaven. The dark night is a means to purify, to cleanse the soul from sin, and infuse it with the Spirit of God. The measure of this infusing, the degree to which we are cleansed, is known only to God. How He chooses to use us in the process is for Him to know. Each saint had a different path to follow, a different mission, a different means of sanctification.

St. Faustina Kowalska

When Jesus spoke to Saint Faustina Kowalska (1905–1938) in 1935, He gave her this mission, "You will prepare the world for My final coming."[18] From this mission came the Divine Mercy prayer and novena, the Divine Mercy image and the diary of St. Faustina. Those consecrated to the Divine Mercy, Jesus Himself, understand the necessity of sacrifice to appease the wrath of God against sin. They also understand that before God's justice is His mercy. He seeks souls that will offer themselves for others, by taking on the consequences of another's sin through the offering of their own suffering. The offering, united to the Sacrifice of the Cross, can give mercy to those being prayed for. "My sacrifice is nothing in itself, but when I join it to the sacrifice of Jesus Christ, it becomes all-powerful and has the power to appease divine wrath."[19]

In this mission of mercy, St. Faustina experienced many blessings and hardships. She came to understand the necessity of suffering needed to accomplish the divine mission of God. Jesus warns her, but comforts her also, "Apostle of My mercy, proclaim to the world My unfathomable mercy. Do not be discouraged by the difficulties you encounter in proclaiming My mercy. These difficulties that affect you so painfully are needed for your sanctification and as evidence that this work is Mine."[20]

Her greatest fear was not being able to accomplish this task, that she would fail in her weaknesses and faith. Jesus, understanding this, reassured her, as He does all those who seek Him. "Do not fear; I, Myself, will make up for everything that is lacking in you."[21] Jesus continues, "Know that I am with you; I bring about the difficulties, and I overcome them. In one instant, I can change a hostile disposition to one which is favorable."[22]

In her journey to do His will, St. Faustina experienced many dark nights when her soul was empty and could not see the face of Jesus. Knowing this caused her more suffering, He reassured her in the manner only God can. "My child, you please Me most by suffering. In your physical as well as your mental sufferings, My daughter, do not seek sympathy from creatures. I want the fragrance of your suffering to be pure and unadulterated. I want you to detach yourself, not only from creatures, but also from yourself."[23]

It was through her sufferings in the dark night, in the detachment of herself she would find the Divine, pure and unspoiled by her physical and mental senses. This purification could only be accomplished through the dark night. It was the means by which Jesus, through her suffering, could save lost souls.

Gradually, as did Mother Teresa, St. Faustina understood that her condition of pain and darkness was needed to bring mercy to others, that the life of redemptive suffering was both costly and fulfilling, yet necessary to bring salvation. As the Passion of our Lord accomplished the greater will of the Father, so she was completing what was lacking in the afflictions of Christ for the church by bringing to the Father her suffering for others and God's mercy with it. Her dark night had a purpose; it brought His light to others.

Her reward for obedience: "My daughter, know that you give Me greater glory by a single act of obedience than by long hours and mortifications."[24]

In the end, she submitted herself to the will of the Father. "I understood that nothing could resist or nullify the will of God. I understood that I must carry out this will of God despite obstacles, persecutions and sufferings of all kinds and despite natural repugnance and fear."[25]

In Her Own Words

Jesus gave me to understand how a soul should be faithful to prayer despite torments, dryness, and temptations; because oftentimes the realization of God's great plans depends mainly on such prayer. If we do not persevere in such prayer, we frustrate what the Lord wanted to do through us or within us.[26]

Nothing is as constant as suffering. It always faithfully keeps the soul company.[27]

Suffering is a great grace; through suffering the soul becomes like the Savior; in suffering, love becomes crystalized; the greater the suffering, the purer the love.[28]

Now I must battle together with Jesus, work with Jesus, suffer with Jesus; in a word, live and die with Jesus.[29]

There is but one price at which souls are bought, and that is suffering, united to My suffering on the Cross.[30]

I have need of your sufferings to rescue souls.[31]

* * * * *

The history of the dark night is old as the story of mankind.

Scripture is filled with Old and New Testament saints who have known hardship and trial. Trials of faith and persecution describe most of the men and women of the Bible, each living the test of faith while doing God's work. The ultimate dark night was the trial of our Lord as He lived out His Passion.

He, too, offered "prayers and supplications with loud cries and tears to the one who was able to save Him from death, and He was heard because of His reverence. Son, though He was, He learned obedience from what He suffered." (Hebrews 5:7–8). Our Lord suffered the same human temptations to disbelieve, to walk away from what the Father is asking of us. Although Son of God, He was tried in His humanity as we all are—in the Night of Darkness. To say the Father left Him in His suffering, or Mary, as she watched her Son die, is unthinkable.

Padre Pio writes,

> Remember what took place in the heart of our heavenly Mother at the foot of the Cross. She was turned to stone before Her crucified Son, due to the excessive suffering, but you cannot say she was abandoned. On the contrary, she was never loved more than at that moment when she suffered and couldn't even cry.[32]

Our Mother's dark night was a living nightmare. But through her Immaculate Conception, she did not sin, not like we who doubt in our nights. Still, the Father did not spare Her. The thoughts of God are higher than our thoughts, sometimes incomprehensible. Both Jesus and His mother have known the dark night—the absence of the Father's presence—and are able to help us along our way.

Dark Night in Our Soul

The dark night is a two-sided coin made of faith and trial. Its purpose is to diminish who we are in nature, to allow the nature of God to grow. It is the process of purification whereby God uses trial to test what we believe in faith. The trial is always equal to the faith required to overcome. No trial is beyond what faith we do have. It was Jesus who said there is no temptation given to man beyond what he is able to endure. Faith is strengthened when endured, which brings the infusing of the Holy Spirit into our life. Faith is always a choice, although a difficult one. Having endured the trial (dark night), we rest until the next one. As our faith increases, so does the intensity of our trials, but with it His presence. It is a lifetime process of trial and faith, until we are purified and made completely into His image. In this dark night is suffering, which Jesus, Mary, and the saints tell us to offer as a sweet, smelling incense, a broken heart He will not deny (Psalm 51).

St. Padre Pio of Pietrelcina

No person of God, no matter how great, holy, or close to God, can escape the dark night. Every person must be tried, purified, and set aside in the great work of salvation.

Padre Pio (1887–1968), Capuchin monk of San Giovanni Rotondo, Italy, is the only Catholic priest to have the stigmata—the five wounds of Christ. Living in both the spiritual and earthly worlds simultaneously, his knowledge and understanding of God and man gave great insight into the spiritual battle between good and evil. His life helped steer others in the ways of God and avoid the pitfalls so many of us fall into. The principles he lived help us in our walk. Padre Pio, who bore the wounds of Christ, had many, many dark nights.

In his darkest times, Padre Pio faced great suffering and bore physical illnesses such as extremely high fevers, nausea, and vomiting which prohibited him from eating and drinking for weeks. He endured respiratory illnesses and spiritual torments from demons who left physical marks on his body. He experienced the scourging and the crown of thorns. His most painful injury was the shoulder wound born by Christ when He carried the Cross. His wounds bled more from Thursday to late Saturday—the time of the Passion. His greatest spiritual and physical sacrifice was the offering of himself in the sacrifice of the Mass. St. Pio was known to experience the full Passion of Christ from the garden of Gethsemane to the crucifixion. His whole life was a living sacrifice consecrated to Christ to bear the consequences of other's sins—*to sanctify himself and sanctify others.*

In his soul, his greatest torment was never having the assurance he was saved, that he was pleasing God and not sinning against Him. It was "an endless desert of darkness, despondency, and insensibility, a land of death, a night of abandonment, a cavern of desolation, in which my poor soul finds itself far from God and alone with itself."[33]

The church sanctioned Padre Pio many times over his wounds, popularity, length of Mass, and rumors of infidelity. In his despondency, he wrote one of his greatest prayers, *Stay with Me, Lord,* to be prayed after Communion.

Padre Pio understood this dark night was not a punishment, but a purgation of the soul in preparation of meeting with its Creator. He understood the necessity of suffering to expiate the sin in his life as he sought to sanctify others. The dark night would change the very nature of the soul. It is the circumcision of the heart—the circumcision of the soul.

> The Lord, your God, will circumcise your hearts and the hearts of your descendants, so that you will love the Lord, your God, with your whole heart and your whole being, in order that you may live. (Deuteronomy 30:6).

Early in his life, Padre Pio sought full union with Christ to help carry His cross. He understood this union to be complete when he was given the wounds of Christ. Through the intercessory life of Padre Pio, we can begin to live the redemptive life through penance and reparation, suffering and sacrifice, and move the heart of God in our dark night. Our wounds are not stigmatic, but they are real as the pain we suffer in life. As St. Pio offered his wounds and suffering for others' sanctification, we can help others remove, or at best, help carry their pain as they walk along the dark path.

Many testified to the suffering of Padre Pio in the Mass and in his life. Bishop Giuseppe Petralia wrote,

> Padre Pio's Mass was a mission of reparation. During the Mass, he relived the tragedy of the Passion in his own body. Padre Pio was made to suffer the agony of Gethsemane, the scourging in the praetorium, the crowning with thorns, the mockery of the crowd, the humiliation of the unjust sentence, the carrying of the Cross, and the crucifixion.[34]

In April 1948, Karol Wojtyla, the future St. Pope John Paul II, attended Padre Pio's Mass. He reflected: "It was long. He was suffering profoundly. On the altar, at San Giovanni Rotondo, the sacrifice of Christ himself, the bloodless sacrifice, was taking place. At the same time, the bloody wounds on the hands of Padre Pio made me think of the whole sacrifice, of Jesus crucified."[35]

In regards to his health, he was at the point of death many times. Padre Rosario da Aliminusa: "Padre Pio always seemed to be at the extreme limits of his strength, and perpetually at the point of death."[36]

Rev. Bernard Ruffin:

> Fra Pio was plagued by a variety of ill-defined physical problems from the very beginning of his novitiate. He suffered from internal intestinal irritability and attacks of vomiting so intense that he was sometimes unable to retain food for weeks on end. Once, for a space of six months, he was forced to subsist largely on milk. He suffered from spasms of violent coughing, was tormented by headaches, and frequently ran high temperatures. Several times he was sent home to try to regain his health. Repeatedly, Fra Pio seemed to be reduced almost to the point of death, only to recover just as suddenly.[37]

Padre Marciano Morra, during a conference at the Casa Sollievo on May 15, 1956, Prof. V. Ewans from London told Padre Carmelo,

> For us doctors, Padre Pio should be biologically dead. A human being simply cannot work so many hours, lose so much blood, and live on such little food, rest, and vacation time. According to the scientific understanding of the basic needs for survival, Padre Pio should be biologically dead.[38]

Asking for this life of suffering, St. Pio would have it no other way. Suffering, for him, whether in his body or spirit, was a means of sanctifying himself and sanctifying others. Through the pain, he was able to bring God's grace into people's lives—in this world and in the next. It was his portion of our Lord's Passion he carried. In Christ, through the Cross, his suffering had purpose and healing.

* * * * *

In His Own Words

> Everything, everything has disappeared from the intelligence, from the soul. An endless desert of darkness, of despondency, of numbness is the birthplace of death, the night of abandonment, the cave of desolation. This is where my poor soul finds itself far from God and all alone.[39]

> An infinite number of fears assail me at every instant. Temptations regarding faith want to drive me to deny everything. My Father, how difficult it is to believe![40]

> The darkness that sometimes surrounds the heaven of your soul is light. Because of this

you think you are in the dark, and you have the impression of being in the center of a burning bush.[41]

Don't let temptations frighten you. They are the trials of those souls whom God wants to put to the test when He sees them strong enough to sustain the battle, weaving with their own hands, the crown of glory.[42]

The angels are jealous of us for one reason only; they are not able to suffer for God. Only through suffering can a soul say with certainty, "My God, You see, I do love You."[43]

Accept all the suffering and incomprehension that comes from Above. In this way you will perfect and sanctify yourself.[44]

I suffer everything that Jesus suffered in the Passion.[45]

The kingdom of Heaven is reached by prayer and suffering.[46]

These are the trials of chosen souls whom God wants to put to the test when he sees they have the necessary strength to sustain the battle.[47]

Rest assured that the more a soul is pleasing to God, the more it must be tried.[48]

Tell our good God to do Himself what you cannot do. Say to Jesus, "Do You want more love from me? I have no more. Give me some more, and I'll offer it to You." Do not doubt. Jesus will accept the offering.[49]

If Jesus manifests Himself, thank Him; and if he hides Himself thank Him also. It is all a game of love. May the clement and pious Virgin continue to obtain for you from the ineffable goodness of the Lord the strength to sustain till the end the many proofs of charity he gives you. I hope you will die with Jesus on the Cross.[50]

* * * * *

Every great saint is touched deeply enough in their dark night to accomplish what God needs to do through them, with them, and in them. We learn submission before we learn to conquer as St. Pio did in his battle with the giant. The length and depth of each Night is determined by its Creator tailored to the soul's condition. His intent is never to punish, but to purify and sanctify. We can do our purification here, or in purgatory. Nothing impure can enter Heaven. As each dark night passes, we move closer to Him in image and holiness, and in our power to intercede for others. Where once our soul was blind, we will see ourselves as He sees, through His eyes. We will learn to trust and obey and love Him with His love in us.

Those who are brave, who trust God beyond humanness, ask Him to allow purgatory in their lives while on earth. Those of lesser faith, in their suffering, feel they are already doing so. Those, like me, live as best they can in the faith that God is presently trying them in love and offer their given sufferings as reparation for sins committed, and for sins committed by others. We ask only that God, in the dark night and circumcision of our soul, be mindful that we are human, lest He bring us to dust (Jeremiah 10:23–24).

Like Padre Pio, through the dark night, He is completing the work He began in us, to sanctify us and sanctify others. This is the way of Christ. This is "the way of Padre Pio."

* * * * *

As for my Bible over the trash can, needless to say, I chose God. It was blind faith—pure choice of the human will. I realized deep within my heart, I had learned to love Him, even when He hurt me, much like family we love. He really is my Father.

> I will never tire of praying to Jesus. It is true that my prayers deserve punishment rather than reward, for I have offended Jesus only too often by my innumerable sins; but, in the end, He will be moved to pity.[51] (Padre Pio)

* * * * *

Battle Plan for the Dark Night[52]

St. Faustina was given instructions from Jesus for her dark nights. We would do well to follow them.

1. Do not fight against the temptation by yourself. Tell your confessor as soon as you can.
2. Do not lose your peace. Live in His presence. Ask Mother Mary and the saints for help.
3. Know that Jesus is looking at you and supporting you.
4. Do not fear the temptation. If you are willing to fight, the victory is always on your side.
5. By fighting, you give Jesus great glory and build merits for yourself. Temptation gives the opportunity to show your fidelity to Christ.

1   Pio, 2003, p. 111.
2   Ruffin, p.106.
3   Teresa, p. 98.
4   Ibid, p. 250.
5   Ibid, p. 233.
6   Ibid, p. 212.
7   Ibid, p. 210.
8   Ibid, p. 225.
9   Ibid, p. 238.
10 Ibid, p. 227.
11 Ibid, p. 248.
12 Ibid, p. 220.
13 Ibid, p. 208.
14 Ibid, p. 157.
15 Ibid, p. 230
16 Lewis, pp. 9–10.
17 Ibid, p. 10.
18 Michalenko, p. 100 (#429).
19 Ibid, p. 110.
20 Ibid, p.179 (#1142).
21 Ibid, p. 101 (#435).
22 Ibid, p. 143 (#788).
23 Ibid, p. 74 (#279).
24 Ibid, p. 156 (#894).
25 Ibid, p. 128.
26 Kowalska, p. 341 (#872).
27 Michalenko, p. 61.
28 Ibid, p.55.
29 Ibid, p.59.
30 Ibid, p. 80 (#324).
31 Ibid, p.242 (#1612).
32 Pio, 2018, p. 88.
33 Ruffin, p.105.
34 Ingoldsby, p.99–100.
35 Castelli, 2011, p. 70–71.
36 Napolitano, 1979, p. 99.
37 Ruffin, p. 67.
38 Morcaldi, 2013, pp. 243–244.
39 Pio, 2003, p. 111.
40 Ibid, p. 117.
41 Pio, 2018, p. 79.
42 Ibid, p. 66.

[43] Ibid, p. 57.
[44] Ibid, p. 58.
[45] Chiron, p. 230.
[46] Napolitano, p. 95.
[47] Pio, 1999, p. 94.
[48] Ibid, p. 38.
[49] Ibid, p. 159.
[50] Pio, 2018, p. 85.
[51] Ibid, p. 29.
[52] Michalenko, p. 233 (#1561).

Perfect Prayer Partner (Purgatory)

The prayers of the souls in Purgatory are much more
efficacious before God, because they pray while suffering.[1]

—Padre Pio

Looking for a prayer partner who is always there for you and never sleeps? Do you need someone who understands your suffering and only wants God's will for you? I have the perfect prayer partner! They pray night and day, seven days a week. They pray for your well-being, spiritual growth, and protection. Their prayers are pure, born from suffering. They pray while suffering, with suffering, and from suffering. Their prayers are what God wants them to pray. They are in the place God wants them to be, doing what He wants them to do. They are the Holy Souls of purgatory. They will not enter Paradise until they have been purified of their sinful nature, for "nothing unclean will enter it, nor any[one] who does abominable things or tells lies. Only those will enter whose names are written in the Lamb's book of life" (Revelation 21:27).

The Catholic Code of Canon Law states purgatory as,

> All who die in God's grace and friendship, but still imperfectly purified, are indeed assured of their eternal salvation; but after death they undergo purification, so as to achieve the holiness necessary to enter the joy of heaven. (CCC 1030)

The saints have left us many descriptions of purgatory, each description tailored to the nature of the sins purified, with the length and depth of each torment determined by the sinful nature that caused it. St. Teresa of Avila (1515–1582), upon falling back on a promise to God leading toward a life away from Him, sent her a vision of purgatory.

> I found myself, as I thought, plunged right into Hell. I realized that it was the Lord's will that I should see the place which the devils had prepared for me there and which I had merited for my sins. This happened in the briefest space of time, but, even if I were to live for many years, I believe it would be impossible for me to forget it. The entrance, I thought, resembled a very long, narrow passage, like a furnace, very low, dark and closely confined; the ground seemed to be full of water which looked like filthy, evil-smelling mud, and in it were many wicked-looking reptiles. At the end there was a hollow place scooped out of a wall, like a cupboard, and it was here that I found myself in close confinement. But the sight of all this was pleasant by comparison with what I felt there… My feelings, I think, could not possibly be exaggerated, nor can anyone understand them. I felt a fire within my soul, the nature of which I am utterly incapable of describing… I had been put in this place which looked like a hole in the wall, and those very walls, so terrible to the sight, bore down upon me and completely stifled me. There was no light and everything was in the blackest darkness.
>
> [T]his vision was one of the most signal favors which the Lord has bestowed upon me; it has been of the greatest benefit to me, both in taking from me all fear of the tribulations and disappointments of this life and also in strength-

ening me to suffer them and to give thanks to the Lord, Who, as I now believe, has delivered me from such terrible and never-ending torments.

It also inspired me with fervent impulses for the good of souls: for I really believe that, to one of them from such dreadful tortures, I would willingly die many deaths. After all, if we see anyone on earth who is especially dear to us suffering great trial or pain, our very nature seems to move us to compassion, and if his sufferings are severe, they oppress us, too."[2]

St. Faustina tells us there are seven torments that are equal to the torments of hell. They are as follows: the loss of God, a remorse of conscience, knowledge your torment will never change, a spiritual fire that penetrates the soul, a continual darkness with a suffocating smell that still allows the devils and the souls of the dammed to see each other with all their evil, the constant company of Satan, and last, an eternal despair and hatred of God.

In this, St. Faustina warns us hell is where the sinner will be tormented throughout eternity with the senses they used to sin with. Jesus responds to this with "My mercy does not want this, but My justice demands it."[3]

The Holy Souls of purgatory are grateful for four things. First, they have the knowledge they are saved and will see God face-to-face; second, they will be purified, and thus enter Heaven undefiled; third, they are thankful for the prayers of the church on their behalf, the greatest prayer being the Holy Mass; last, they are thankful for the visits of Mother Mary who brings them refreshment. The souls in purgatory call her "the Star of the Sea,"[4] remembering her promise to those who wear her scapular during life, to free them from purgatory the first Saturday after their death. She is truly Mother of Mercy. The saints also tell us we are also visited by our guardian angel while we are in purgatory.

* * * * *

Padre Pio, who offered himself for souls in purgatory, not only had an intimate knowledge of who was there, but also would visit the souls. When told by a spiritual daughter to ask St. Francis on his feast day to release her parents from purgatory, he replied he could do it himself.

He had knowledge and experience of what the souls endured and often compared his suffering with those in purgatory. When asked about the fires of purgatory, Padre Pio answered, "If the Lord were to give permission to the soul to pass from that fire (of purgatory) to the greatest fire on earth, it would be like passing from hot water to cool water."[5]

St. Pio knew the praying power of the souls in purgatory and understood the influence our prayers and sacrifices had in the release of souls from purgatory. He offered Mass for souls in purgatory knowing the Mass is the most powerful intercession, sacrifice, and expiation for anyone, any sin, anytime, anywhere.

Padre Alessio Parente, an assistant of Padre Pio, tells this story of those helped by Padre Pio's masses:

> One night in 1944, the friars heard loud voices coming from downstairs saying, "Viva Padre Pio." The superior Padre Raffaele da S. Elia, a Pianisi, told the doorkeeper Fra Gerardo da Deliceto to escort the people out and to lock the door securely. Fra Gerardo went downstairs, but there was nobody to be seen. When he checked, the door was double locked as it was supposed to be. He went back to report on what he had seen. Padre Raffaele was puzzled and went straight to Padre Pio asking if he knew anything about what was going on. Padre Pio said to him: "Oh! They were a group of soldiers who had died on the battlefield, and came here to thank me for my prayers for their salvation."[6]

Padre Pio was once asked, "Padre, how can I suffer purgatory here on earth so I can go straight to heaven immediately?" He replied, "By accepting everything from God's hands. By offering everything up to Him with love and thanksgiving so as to enable us to pass from our death-bed to Paradise."[7] Our Lord uses the troubles of this world to purify us.

The ministry of St. Pio was twofold, help those on earth in their journey with God and help those in purgatory attain Heaven. The offer of his suffering to Christ in the Mass—his wounds, his physical and spiritual torments—served as expiation and reparation for those he prayed for.

We cannot offer to God what St. Pio offered to the degree he did. As he said, not all were called as he was. We can only offer ourselves in the condition we are in, with what God brings and allows into our lives. Our wounds may not be the physical wounds on our hands, feet, and side; but the pain we feel is real—even unto death.

And what can we offer the poor souls? Padre Alessio Parente, one of Padre Pio's many assistants, in his book *The Holy Souls*, tells us,

> So, what are the basic conditions necessary to offer good works for the Holy Souls?
>
> 1. The good works should be carried out in a reverential manner and without ulterior motives, because only in this way will the Lord make recompense.
> 2. The good work should be carried out in a state of grace, because when the soul is in a state of mortal sin, it cannot make satisfaction either for itself or for others.
> 3. When we carry out a good work for the Poor Souls, it is necessary to have the intention of applying it either to them in general, or to some soul in particular,

or to a category of souls, for example,
the souls of the poor, and so forth.[8]

He continues on with good works to include fasting, giving alms, self-denial, and most importantly, accepting every suffering as from God. And of course, offering the Mass for the Holy Souls is the greatest prayer. It is comforting to know Padre Pio, as our spiritual father, will stand with us when we stand before the Father for judgment and fight for us if we are unfortunate to spend time in purgatory as he fought for the holy souls when he was on earth.

Padre Alessio Parente, one of Padre Pio's many assistants, in his book *The Holy Souls*, tells the story of St. Gertrude (1256–1301). She is often invoked for the souls in purgatory.

> On her death-bed, Saint Gertrude was berated by the devil for having used the merits of her good works and sacrifices for the benefit of the Holy Souls in Purgatory. The devil tempted her, accusing her of not having thought enough of herself. He told her that she had been stupid for not having obtained the merits of her sufferings for herself, since she was greatly in need. "Who do you think you are?" the devil said to her, "to offer up your daily prayers and sacrifices for souls whom you don't even know. You will soon keenly regret this error, while I laugh. You will pay dearly for this mistake."
>
> On hearing this, Saint Gertrude was greatly disturbed, and she thought of the great suffering that awaited her. But the Lord did not want to see His faithful servant in such a state, so He appeared to her and said, "My daughter, why are you so upset? You should know that your charity was greatly appreciated by Me, so that I now release you from whatever suffering has been prescribed for you. And as I have promised a great

reward for those who offer themselves for the salvation of their brothers and sisters, so your joy in Heaven will be increased a hundredfold. All those souls whom you have saved will meet you shortly to bring you into Paradise."

When she heard all this, the saintly virgin told everything to those who surrounded her, and with a smile on her lips, she went to her eternal reward.[9]

Queen of Purgatory

As mentioned, Mother Mary is known as the Star of the Sea among the Holy Souls. It is important to know this because it will benefit us when we are there as she does even more.

Our Lady of Carmel has promised those who wear her scapular release from purgatory the first Saturday after their death. The promises given to St. Dominic to those who pray the Rosary include release from purgatory. St. Damian writes that on the feast day of Assumption, Mary frees many souls.[10] Who knows on how many other feast days she may descend to free souls. It would benefit us greatly to know this Queen even better.

* * * * *

As we offer reparation for loved ones here on earth, we must also remember those who have passed, as we hope and pray that those alive *will remember us* when we have passed. St. Pio said our prayers are never wasted. When those we pray for in purgatory pass onto heaven, our continued prayers will be used for others still present there. We benefit threefold: we assist in the release of souls from purgatory into Heaven, we invoke the prayers and intercession of countless souls who know no boundary in time and space when praying for those who sacrifice for them, and we may just shave off a little of our time in purgatory.

As God knows no boundaries in time and space, I often say a prayer for myself.

In His Own Words

More souls of the dead from purgatory than of the living climb this mountain to attend my Masses and seek my prayers.[11]

The souls in purgatory don't suffer more than I do.[12]

We need to pray for the souls in purgatory. We have yet to comprehend how much they can do for us, through the gratitude they have for those who pray for them![13]

The souls in purgatory pray for us, and their prayers are even more effective than ours, because they are accompanied by their suffering. So, let's pray for them, and let's pray them to pray for us… The souls in Purgatory repay the prayers that we say for them… When we pray for the souls in Purgatory, we will always get something back.[14]

"Tomorrow is the feast of St. Francis. Please ask him to go to Purgatory and free the souls of my parents." Padre Pio replied: "I can do it myself."[15]

[1]   Parente, 2011, p. 110.

[2]   Avila, chapter 32, parts 1–9.

[3]   Michalenko, p. 31 (#20).

[4]   Ibid, p. 31.

[5]   Parente, 2015, p. 46.

[6] Parente, 2011, p. 56.
[7] Parente, 2015, pp. 62–63.
[8] Ibid, p. 115.
[9] Ibid, pp.114–115.
[10] Ibid, p. 108.
[11] Ibid, pp. 69–70.
[12] Parente, 2011, p. 259.
[13] Ibid, pp. 109–110.
[14] Ibid, pp. 108–109.
[15] Parente, 2015, p. 70.

Living the Redemptive Life

I am saying this that you may constantly unite yourself with
Me through love, for this is the goal of the life of your soul.[1]
—Jesus to St. Faustina

I have never been one to do things half-heartedly. I am in it all the
way, or I am not. My Christian life is this way. There are those who
say, "All things in moderation." Well, if I pray in moderation, will
the Lord answer me in moderation? If I tithe moderately, will He
bless me moderately? If God were to give me as I give Him, I would
be living in a shanty, cold, in want of the basic things in life. When
people comment on my retired life from education, the blessings of
my children, and our health, I say, "The only difference between you
and me is I have learned to say yes to God."

There are the things we do for God, and there are the things
God tells us to do. I have learned and am learning the difference. I
am not looking for things to fill my life. I am asking God to fill it
with His will—every moment of my life. Not in moderation. Our
life here is short. How short? I will illustrate.

Imagine a sphere as large as our sun. This sphere is made of
Vibranium (yes, from Wakanda). Now imagine a dove landing lightly
on this sphere only to fly away returning every thousand years. How
long would it take for this sphere to wear down? That is the beginning of eternity. Our time on this earth is likened to the one touch of
the dove on the sphere. What is the importance of this touch? It will
determine how our time in eternity is spent. There are no do-overs.

Every moment, every action, every thought has eternal meaning and consequences, one hundred percent of the time.

We are offered glances into what lies ahead, directions to our destination. For the spiritual children of Padre Pio, we have his way and his help, "Give me Friday and I'll give you the whole week."[2]

If we are to live the life of sacrifice and suffering through penance and reparation, we must ask Jesus what it is He asks of us. It is as different for me as we are different from one another. What He asks of me may or may not be what He asks of you. Not everyone is called to be a Victim Soul, but we are all called to be Chosen Souls. Our response is to say yes to Him. How do we know what it is He is asking of us? There lies the beginning of *the way.*

Nothing happens, but first prayer.

Let me illustrate.

When I met my wife, we talked a lot. We talked at work where we met; we talked at dinner. We talked before the movies and after the movies. We talked at the coffee shop. I always believed I would marry the woman whose company I enjoyed over a cup of coffee and good conversation. We talked, and we listened. We began to understand where God was in each other's lives. In the end, we fell in love with each other. And God used her to bring me back to Catholicism.

So it is with God. Every good relationship begins with talking and listening. And if you are like me, no relationship is half-hearted. If time with God begins with prayer, begin with the Mass. There is no greater prayer. As St. Faustina said, Communion is the beginning of spending eternity with God. The Mass is a conversation between God and man. It is a prayer of speaking and listening. The conversation centers on this: the priest speaks the words "This is my Body which is given up for you." We respond, "My Lord and my God." For St. Pio, participation in the Mass was his greatest and most difficult expression of God's love in his life as he participated physically and spiritually with Christ in His Passion. *Listen* to the Mass. Better yet, *participate!* The graces received will overwhelm you.

Every action has eternal value. Every thought has redemption, if offered up to His good purpose. In prayer, we offer all things to Him; we avoid the devil's trap Eve fell into—doubting God and following our own will. In every circumstance, we are moving toward God, or away. St. Pio commented on the Christian life, "One must always go forward and never back in the spiritual life. When a boat stops, instead of going forward the wind blows it back."[3] In his book, *My Utmost for Highest*, Oswald Chambers states, "The things that happen either make us fiends, or they make us saints."[4] In all things, "God will not leave us alone until we are one with Him."[5] In offering all things to Him, He removes what is not of Himself from our life. Like the making of petrified wood, what is degradable—our soul— is slowly replaced with mineral and sediment—His Spirit—until all that was natural is now solid stone—heavenly armament—unaffected by the elements of life. We begin to take the form of Christ as He lives through us in our thoughts and in our actions, in our prayers and suffering. Jesus will create in us the image of Himself to the degree we allow it! It begins with prayer!

In all matters, pray. In all circumstances, pray. When in doubt, listen and pray. Allow silence when you are frustrated; allow quiet when you have nothing say. Prayer places us in the presence of God. Be present before Him. Without prayer, we are adrift on a boat with no oars. Prayer is the beginning of the Redemptive Life, the beginning of knowing His will for us.

How do we get the most out of this life and the next with prayer? How do we begin to live the redemptive life and knowing His will? *By accepting what God allows in our life and offering it back to Him for His good purpose.* Whether it is the stuff of life, the temptation of Satan, or the intervention of God, when placed in His Hands, the action we offer here on earth becomes our crown in heaven. This is the same crown offered St. Pio when Christ told him he would have to fight the giant all his life but in the end would receive a crown of glory.

The church has direction for us in this matter. We are not without battle armaments in this spiritual warfare. Here are church-sanctioned devotions and prayers we can use to know His will and seek help for others.

Vocal Prayers/Devotions

Prayers

- Rosary
- Chaplet of Divine Mercy
- Morning Offering
- First Thursdays Devotion / Act of Reparation to the Wounds of Jesus
- First Friday Devotion / Act of Reparation to the Sacred Heart of Jesus
- First Saturdays Devotion / Act of Reparation to the Immaculate Heart of the Blessed Virgin Mary
- Rosary of the Holy Wounds
- Novenas to Mary
- Novenas to Jesus
- Novenas to saints
- Novenas to special days

Opportunities for Meditation/Reparation

- Time of prayer and/or Adoration before the Blessed Sacrament
- Confession
- Mass: offer those prayed for in the intentions of the Mass
- Pilgrimages
- Fasting
- Honoring feast days through prayer and fasting
- Visiting a cemetery to pray for passed loved ones
- Charity
- Tithe

When offering an act of reparation, begin with the Prayer of Fatima:

> O Jesus, it is for Your love, for the conversion of sinners, and in reparation for the sins committed against the Immaculate Heart of Mary.[6]

When offering the prayer of intercession during Mass, follow the words of Jesus to St. Faustina and pray this during the act of consecration. This may also be prayed at any time for another soul. Jesus to St. Faustina:

> Father, I offer the Body, the Blood, the Soul and Divinity of Your dearly beloved Son, our Lord Jesus Christ, in atonement for the sins of __________.[7]

The Mass offers the greatest form of reparation, prayer and meditation because it is His sacrifice for us. In the tradition of tapping the heart with a clenched fist during each chime of the bell that signifies the presence of God in His Body and Blood, I unite my body, my blood, my soul and life with His on the Cross. Thereby, all that I am is given to Him. I make my life a reparation offering united to His sacrifice on the Cross.

* * * * *

In living the Redemptive Life, we place all we do in His Hands, every second of every day, thereby bringing redemption to all we do and to all we pray for. Padre Pio reminds us how short this life is and what we are accountable for:

> We truly have done nothing to date, or perhaps, very little; the years have followed one another and from beginning to end, we have never asked ourselves how we have spent them,

whether there was something to be rectified, to be added or obliterated from our conduct. We have lived thoughtlessly, as if the Eternal Judge were not going to call us to Himself one day and ask us to account for our deeds and for the way we have spent our time. And yet, we must give an exact account of every moment, of every grace, of every holy inspiration, of every opportunity to do good. The slightest transgression of God's holy laws will be taken into consideration![8]

How do we live the Redemptive Life? *By praying to accept what God allows in our life and offering it back to Him for His good purpose, for love of Jesus, for the conversion of sinners, and in reparation for the sins committed against the Immaculate Heart of Mary.* We become a living sacrifice of love, reparable souls, and great will be our power of intercession for those we love. Isn't that what it is all about? Our only limitations for intercessory prayer will be our limit to love and willingness to suffer. When in doubt what to pray or what to offer in times of great distress, pray, "Lord, take from me what You need. If I do not have it, give it to me so I can give it to You. Help me embrace You on the Cross."

Nothing happens but, first, prayer.

In His Own Words

Do not start any activity without first offering it to God.[9]

One day the slightest transgression of god's law will be considered.[10]

Before going to sleep, examine your conscience and turn your thoughts to God.[11]

God is always fixed in my mind and imprinted in my heart.[12]

Time spent for the glory of God is never wasted.[13]

The kingdom of heaven is reached by prayer and suffering.[14]

Be constant and persevering. The prize will be given to the one who brings things to completion, not to the one who starts and then stops.[15]

Everybody should understand the preciousness of time. Let us treasure every instant. Only the passing moment is in our power. One day we will have to give a strict account of every minute.[16]

Let us not delay till tomorrow what we can do today. How can we be sure that tomorrow we will still be alive?[17]

Do not care about tomorrow. Do good deeds today. And when tomorrow comes, it will become your today, and then you can care about it.[18]

He who begins to love must be ready to suffer.[19]

* * * * *

More Words on Redemptive Life

Suffering is a great grace; through suffering the soul becomes like the Savior; in suffering love becomes crystallized; the greater the suffering, the purer the love.[20] (Jesus to St. Faustina)

My beloved daughter, you have come to know well the depths of My mercy. I will do what you ask, but unite yourself continually with My agonizing Heart and make reparation to My justice. Know that you have asked Me for great thing, but I see that this was dictated by your pure love for Me; that is why I am complying with your requests.[21] (Jesus to St. Faustina)

You are not living for yourself but for souls, and other souls will profit from your sufferings. Your prolonged suffering will give them the light and strength to accept My will.[22] (Jesus to St. Faustina)

Do you see these souls? Those are like Me in the pain and contempt they suffer will be like Me also in glory. And those who resemble Me less in pain and contempt will also bear less resemblance to Me in glory.[23] (Jesus to St. Faustina)

Pray, pray very much; and make sacrifice for sinners. Many souls are lost, because there are none to make sacrifices for them.[24] (Virgin Mary to children at Fatima)

Mental prayer is nothing else than an intimate friendship, a frequent heart-to-heart conversation with Him by whom we know ourselves to be loved.[25] (St. Teresa of Avila)

He who neglects mental prayer needs not a devil to carry him to hell, but he brings himself there with his own hands.[26] (St. Teresa of Avila)

Know, dearest daughter, how, by humble, continual, and faithful prayer, the soul acquires, with time and perseverance, every virtue.[27] (St. Catherine of Siena)

By means of humble and continuous prayer, founded on knowledge of herself and of God… prayer…unites with God the soul that follows the footprints of Christ crucified, and thus, by desire and affection, and union of love, makes herself another Himself.[28] (St. Catherine of Siena)

Perfect prayer is not attained through many words, but through affection of desire, the soul raising herself to Me, with knowledge of herself and My mercy.[29] (St. Catherine of Siena)

Holy desire is a continuous prayer.[30] (St. Catherine of Siena)

Whatever he may contribute, by word or deeds, towards the salvation of his neighbor, is virtually a prayer.[31] (St. Catherine of Siena)

Every exercise, whether performed, in oneself or in one's neighbor, with good-will, is prayer.[32] (St. Catherine of Siena)

She will know herself in humble and continuous prayer and holy and true desire.[33] (St. Catherine of Siena)

1   Kowalska, pp. 243–244 (#576).
2   Tangari, p. 140.
3   Pio, 2018, pp.15–16.
4   Chambers, May 22.
5   Ibid.
6   McGlynn, p. 204.
7   Kowalska, p. 20 (#39).
8   Pio, 2018, pp. 6–7.
9   Epistolario IV, p. 450.
10 Padre Pio, 2010, p. 7.
11 Pio, 2010, pp. 147–148.
12 Epistolario I, p. 1247.
13 Padre Pio, 2010, p. 172.
14 Napolitano, 1979, p. 95.
15 Morcaldi, 2013, pp. 216.
16 Padre Pio, 2010, p. 5.
17 Ibid., p. 4.
18 Epistolario IV, p. 437.
19 Padre Pio, 2010, p. 51.
20 Kowalska, p. 29 (#57).
21 Ibid, p. 341 (#873).
22 Ibid, p. 34 (#67).
23 Ibid, p. 197 (#446).
24 McGlynn, p. 204.
25 Rohrbach, p. 3.
26 Ibid, p. 7.
27 Catherine, p. 92.
28 Ibid, p. 1.
29 Ibid, p. 96.
30 Ibid, p. 96.
31 Ibid, p. 96.
32 Ibid, p. 97.
33 Ibid, p. 38.

How Then Shall We Live?

*The ecstasies and the apparitions began at the young
age of five, when he first had the desire to consecrate
himself to the Lord, and they were continuous.*[1]
—Padre Agostino Daniele

I have come to believe there are souls given a sensitivity to God at birth. They are sensitive to His ways and tend to believe the things of God easier. I am one of them. By the age of five, I knew in my soul God existed. My actions as a youth were governed by a sense of what He wanted of me. As a teen, I was reading my Bible and praying. For a fifteen-year-old, that says a lot. Whether it was girls, parties, or spending time reading my Bible, I knew what was right and what was wrong. I felt directed toward helping others in my young adulthood and felt led to attend a Bible college for training. I believed whatever occupation I chose, a strong knowledge of Scripture was necessary to get along in life. It has made all the difference.

Saint Pio was one of those sensitive souls close to our Lord and Mother Mary from a very young age. Visions of both were common to him. He spoke with his guardian angel often and believed everyone could see and speak with theirs. Heavenly experiences were normal to him. Padre Pio knew his heavenly calling early unlike many of us who only have inclinations toward God and His leading in our life. Throughout the history of the church, saints received a specific calling to their mission in life through a yearning or *thirst* for something or someone. This calling, or *sitio* in Latin, is a thirst, a yearning for something.

This pattern was repeated in the lives of the saints. Whether early in life or late, each had a sense of direction, a calling or sitio for what they felt God was asking of them. As we search for our place in living the redemptive life, let us look at the lives of the Spiritual Giants who answered the call to sanctify themselves and sanctify others.

* * * * *

For Saint Faustina (1905–1938), her *sitio* came from our Lord, "I want to see you as a *living sacrifice of love,* which only then carries weight before Me…and great will be your power for whomever you intercede."[2] With this, she would understand the words, "Help Me, My daughter, to save souls. Join your suffering to My Passion and offer them to the Heavenly Father for sinners."[3] This passion of living as a sacrifice of love would lead her to the message of Divine Mercy for the world and prepare it for His second coming.

The *sitio* for Saint Therese of Lisieux (1873–1897) came with the words,

> Yes, My Beloved, this is how my life will be consumed. I have no other means of proving my love for You other than that of strewing flowers, that is, not allowing one little sacrifice to escape, not one look, one word, profiting by all the smallest things and doing them through love.[4]

This sitio became known as her "little way" of showing her love for God in the way duties are performed, prayers are offered, and all of life's actions performed. It allowed God's love to work through her, to do small things with great love.

For Mother Teresa of Calcutta (1910–1987), it was exactly that—"I Thirst." The Charter for the Missionaries of Charity states their mission as "to quench the thirst of our Lord Jesus Christ for the salvation of souls."[5] Her *sitio* was to be His light in the darkness of the Indian slums, "to bring God to souls and souls to God."[6]

The words, "I thirst," were among the seven last sayings Jesus spoke on the Cross before He died. In His humanity, He was thirsty for water. In His deity, He was thirsty for souls. Even in the last moments of His death, He was thinking of us: I offer My Life for yours; I do this because I love you and thirst for your soul to be united to Mine. In His thirst for souls, He was given vinegar.

As we serve our Lord, walking the path of Padre Pio, we must be careful not to give Him vinegar. We must search out our calling to know what He is asking of us, what it is we are yearning. As St. Pio often said, "The Lord asks this of me. He does not ask the same of you."[7] Is it to sacrifice for others? Is it to pray constantly, to start prayer groups, serve as lector, Eucharistic minister, or sacristan? What is it you feel called to do to complete "what is lacking in the afflictions of Christ on behalf of His body, the church?" Your answer may be a lifelong search. You may already know what it is; you just haven't acted on it. Your sitio will guide you along the path of St. Pio.

* * * * *

In this world are many distractions, many "callings" for our soul. They come from the comforts of this world and from the gods of self-pleasure. They call from our egos, from self-reliance, and "all things in moderation." They hinder our search for God, drown out His calling, and prevent us from moving toward Him. We do not grow in Him because we only tolerate His life in us. We offer Him vinegar instead of our lives.

In a letter to the Missionaries of Charity, Mother Teresa writes,

> Until you can hear Jesus in the silence of your own heart, you will not be able to hear Him saying, "I thirst,"... Jesus Himself must be the one to say to you "I thirst." Hear your own name. Not just once. Everyday. If you listen with your heart, you will hear, you will understand... "I thirst" is something much deeper than Jesus just saying, "I love you." Until you know deep

inside that Jesus thirsts for you—you can't begin
to know who He wants to be for you. Or, who
He wants you to be for Him.[8]

Mother Teresa continues,

> I worry some of you still have not really met
> Jesus—one on one—you and Jesus alone. We
> may spend time in Chapel—but have you seen
> with the eyes of your soul how He looks at you
> with love? Do you really know the living Jesus—
> not from book, but from being with Him in
> your heart? Have you heard the loving words He
> speaks to you? Never give up this daily intimate
> contact with Jesus as the real living person—not
> just the idea.[9]

You cannot answer the *sitio* God gives you until you have His
Spirit to hear it. You must speak His language to hear His voice.
Only then can you understand what your *sitio* is and what He is call-
ing you to do. You are giving Jesus vinegar until you do.

The answer to receiving your *sitio* and knowing what it is is
simple: *ask for it*. "You do not possess because you do not ask" (James
4:2). "When you look for me, you will find me. Yes, when you seek
me with all your heart" (Jeremiah 29:13).

* * * * *

How then shall we live? If your answer is "my life is spiritually
lukewarm," "I am inattentive to God," "life is just okay," "keeping
the status quo is fine," you have either not answered your *sitio* or you
do not know what it is. You are giving Jesus vinegar when He wants
to give you Living Water.

Do not answer Jesus with things that don't really matter to you
and cost you nothing. Offer Him what He wants most. The answer
to His call is *you*. Give Him worship and give Him praise. Give Him

your time in prayer, in Adoration, confession, and charitable acts. Give Him your suffering and quench His thirst in you. As St. Pio advises,

> Be totally resigned in the hands of our Lord, giving Him your remaining years, and begging Him always, to fill them with preparations for a life which is pleasing to Him. Don't worry about useless promises of tranquility, enjoyment or merits, but present your hearts to your divine Spouse, totally emptying it of all other affections, except His chaste love.[10]

Hear the words Jesus has for you: "I thirst for you."

* * * * *

Not many can say with certainty as Padre Pio, "From my birth, the Lord showed me signs of a very special predilection."[11]

Having a soul sensitive to God from birth helps. His sitio was to sanctify himself and sanctify others and be a Victim Soul that would take on himself the consequence of sin in a person's life so God could work His grace in them. If you are to live his life of sacrifice, reparation, and penance, you must know your sitio—your calling. As St. Mother Teresa said, you must know Jesus from being in your heart. You cannot move forward in this way of living until you do so.

In our search for His calling in our life, we have a spiritual father who can help us. Padre Pio is waiting for his children. He will help you find your sitio and quench your thirst, to guide you along "the way of Padre Pio."

In His Own Words

> I will take charge of your soul, and you will know the will of God.[12]

I shall be able to do much more for you when I am in heaven than I can now while I am on earth.[13]

Tell the American people that for those who would like me to be their spiritual father, my answer is yes. I accept all Americans as my spiritual children. I only have two requirements—that they lead very good Catholic lives and that they regularly receive the sacraments. And please, tell them never to embarrass me in front of Jesus and Mary.[14]

I have made a pact with the Lord: I will take my place at the gate to Paradise, but I shall not enter until I have seen the last of my spiritual children enter.[15]

You put in your good will and I will take care of the rest of it.[16]

Jesus will assist you and give you the grace to lead a heavenly life and nothing whatever will be able to separate you from His love.[17]

To meet Padre Pio even after his death is to find heaven, because that is where he will lead you.[18] (Fr. Joseph Pius Martin)

The Lord gave me a great mission that is known only to Him and me.[19]

My mission is that of saving souls.[20]

My true mission will begin after my death.[21]

I live only to serve the Heavenly Father: I do not live for myself: only for Him.[22]

Among you, I am your brother. On the Altar, I am your victim. In the confessional, I am your judge.[23]

---

[1] Allen, 2012, p. 25.
[2] Kowalska, p. 627 (#1767).
[3] Ibid, p. 392 (#1032).
[4] Lisieux, p. 196.
[5] Teresa, p. 139.
[6] Ibid, p. 77.
[7] Allen, 2012, p. 38.
[8] "Catholic Life Ministries."
[9] Ibid.
[10] Pio, 2018, pp. 211–212.
[11] Epistolario III, p. 1,006.
[12] Ruffin, p. 64.
[13] Ibid, p. 14.
[14] Allen, 2012, p. 194.
[15] Parente, 2015, p. 65.
[16] Allen, 2011, p. 203.
[17] Ibid, p. 170.
[18] Ibid, p. 22.
[19] Morcaldi, 2013, p. 180.
[20] Iasenzaniro, 2006, p. 9.
[21] Duchess Suanne, 1968, p. 21.
[22] Epistolario I, p. 497.
[23] Chiron, 1999, p. 237.

Biography of Padre Pio

Now I rejoice in my sufferings for your sake, and in my
flesh, I am filling up what is lacking in afflictions of
Christ on behalf of His Body, which is the Church.

—Colossians 1:24

Francesco Forgione (Padre Pio) was born in the small farming town
of Pietrelcina, Italy, on May 25, 1887, to a family of strong Catholic
faith. He was very religious and loved to go to church to pray. He
was five years old when he dedicated his life to God. As a young boy,
Francesco had shown signs of extraordinary gifts of grace. He was not
only able to see and talk with his guardian angel, but also with Jesus
and the Virgin Mary. He thought everyone was able to see and speak
with these heavenly beings.

At the age of fifteen, he was admitted as a novitiate of the
Capuchin Order of the Friars Minor in Morcone, Italy. The students
there noted he was pious, humble, and always in prayer. Padre Pio
was ordained to the priesthood August 10, 1910.

Already feeling a sense of direction and calling as a young priest
to help others, in November of the same year he wrote a letter to his
spiritual director, Father Benedetto Nardella, asking permission to
offer his life as a victim for sinners. Padre Pio wrote,

> For a long time, I have felt in myself a need
> to offer myself to the Lord as a victim for poor
> sinners and for the souls in Purgatory. This desire
> has been growing continually in my heart so that

it has now become what I would call a strong passion…imploring on Him to lay on me the punishments prepared for sinners and for souls in Purgatory so long as He converts and saves sinners and quickly releases the souls in Purgatory. It seems to me that Jesus wants this.[1]

This "calling" to be a victim for souls came after Padre Pio experienced a physical stigmata in September 1910 given to him by Jesus and Mary. The wounds appeared for a short time, then disappeared, but remained as painful sensations. In August 1918, a permanent physical wound on his side was given by a heavenly being using a "long, sharp-pointed steel blade which seemed to spew out fire."[2] This would be known later as the transverberation. These were preparations for what was to come next in answer to his call.

On September 20, 1918, while praying before the crucifix at Our Lady of Grace church, in San Giovanni, Italy, a mysterious celestial being appeared before Padre Pio. Padre Pio recounted the event as such:

> After celebrating Mass, I stayed in the choir for the due thanksgiving prayer, when suddenly I was overtaken by a powerful trembling, then calm followed, and I saw our Lord in the posture of someone who is on a cross (but it didn't strike me whether He had the cross), lamenting the ingratitude of men, especially those consecrated to Him and by Him most favored. This revealed His suffering and His desire to unite souls with His Passion. He invited me to partake of His sorrows and to meditate on them. At the same time, He urged me to work for my brother's salvation. I felt then full of compassion for the Lord's sorrows, and I asked Him what I could do. I heard this voice, "I unite you with My Passion." Once the vision disappeared, I came to, I returned to

my sense, and I saw these signs here, which were dripping blood.[3]

It was then Padre Pio received the physical stigmata—the wounds of Christ—that would stay with him for fifty years. With the stigmata came the gifts of bilocation, reading of consciences, prophecy, healing, gift of conversion, fragrances, languages, communication with angels, and the knowing of past, present, future events as God gave them to him. With these graces came much suffering: flagellations, the crowning of thorns, and a wound of some length on his right shoulder. These were in answer to the Father's call to share in His Son's Passion. They would be the means of reparation and expiation for souls.

As news spread about the priest who bled, many came to San Giovanni Rotondo where Padre Pio lived. It would be several years before the church would sanctify the stigmata and the priest. This process would include several investigations by Vatican-sponsored doctors, priests, and other lay people who would examine the wounds. Rumors of immorality and staging his own wounds would be carried to the Holy See. These investigations and allegations culminated in a period of isolation in which Padre Pio was stripped of all his priestly duties except Mass where he was limited to a one-room chapel with one assistant.

Eventually, church officials would clear Padre Pio of any wrongdoing. His priestly duties would be restored, and the people would again flock to San Giovanni. The faithful continued to be faithful. His morning masses would continue to bless those who attended, many feeling as if heaven were present. His reading of consciences during confession, his healings, and other graces would continue to bring the faithful to San Giovanni. It is now known that St. Pio suffered the Passion of Christ before and during the Mass.

With the Second World War bringing soldiers from all nations to Italy, to San Giovanni, and Our Lady of Grace, Padre Pio's reputation spread across the globe. With his long hours in the confessional, two-hour masses, wounds, and other illnesses, his life was not easy; but it was the sacrificial life he asked for and received. He said of his ills, "Bearing physical and moral ailments is the worthiest offering you can make to He who saved us through suffering."⁴

Saint Pio was always praying the Rosary. He had one sewn into his habit so he could pray continually wherever he was, doing whatever he was doing. When asked by a superior how many rosaries he had prayed that day, he replied with thirty-five up to that point. His sufferings and prayers were offered for both the living on earth and for those in purgatory. He said more souls from purgatory attended his masses than the living, thanking him for a Mass said for them. His motto: "I have regenerated them to Jesus through suffering and love."⁵

He continued to battle hell all his life as demons often attacked him at night. He was often left bloody and bruised. Satan came disguised as clergy, friends, animals, and once as a well-dressed man in the confessional. It wasn't until Padre Pio became suspicious of the man and said, "Say Long live Jesus, long live Mary,"⁶ that the man vanished.

As the Second World War loomed over Europe, the Holy See Pope Pius XII requested prayer for the church and for world peace. This gave way to Pio's request for prayer groups that would both support the hospital and answer the Pontiff's call for prayer. These prayer groups had specific membership requests by Padre Pio:

- To live intensely on God's grace and make use of the sacraments of Eucharist and reconciliation.
- To live one's faith in words and actions, in a true Christian life.
- To love Jesus Christ crucified, the Most Blessed Sacrament, our Blessed Mother, the holy Father, and the Roman Catholic Church.
- To be proactive and animated by a sincere spirit of charity toward all.

The call and mission of every prayer group was to offer to the church and to society the wonderful contribution of continual and confident prayer. The prayer groups are now the International Association of Padre Pio Prayer Groups.

After the War, there was a need for helping the sick. Padre Pio shared a vision where he saw the image of Christ in the poor, the suffering, and the sick, and Christ giving Himself to them. From this vision came the hospital Casa Sollievo della Sofferenza (House of Suffering). Its construction began in 1947 and was completed in 1956. It continues to thrive today and is one of Italy's finest hospitals.

Padre Pio celebrated his last Mass September 22, 1968, and passed onto Heaven September 23, 1968. The Father Guardian stated that within ten minutes of his passing, all marks of the stigmata were gone. He was canonized in 2002. His feast day is celebrated September 23. His body was exhumed in 2008 and entombed at the church of Our Lady of Grace in San Giovanni Rotundo, Italy. Every year, 8 million people visit San Giovanni Rotundo, Italy, to see the saint. He often said, "I will remain at the gates of Paradise; I will go in when I have seen the last of my children enter."[7] "Everyone can say, Padre Pio is mine."[8]

At the canonization of Saint Pio, Pope John Paul II said this about Padre Pio and the prayer groups:

> In fact, the ultimate reason for the apostolic effectiveness of Padre Pio, the profound root of so much spiritual fruitfulness can be found in that intimate and constant union with God, attested to by his long hours spent in prayer and in the confessional. He loved to repeat, "I am a poor Franciscan who prays" convinced that "prayer is the best weapon we have, a key that opens the heart of God."
>
> This fundamental characteristic of his spirituality continues in the 'Prayer Groups' that he founded, which offer to the Church and to society the wonderful contribution of incessant and confident prayer. To prayer, Padre Pio joined an intense charitable activity, of which the 'Home

for the Relief of Suffering' is an extraordinary expression. Prayer and charity, this is the most concrete synthesis of Padre Pio's teaching, which today is offered to everyone.[9]

Padre Pio lived his life of penance and reparation through suffering and sacrifice. A Victim Soul, one given to God for the salvation of the world, was a life of redemptive suffering. He asked the same of his spiritual children.

*****

Among the Protestants is a famous preacher of the late 1800s, Dwight L. Moody of the Moody Institute. Upon departing across the Atlantic Ocean, Moody had these words given to him, "The world has yet to see what God will do with and for and through and in and by the man who is fully and wholly consecrated to Him."[10] If the world had a person totally consecrated to God, what would they look like? What would they sound like? Would they carry the wounds of Christ? Would they know the mind of God and yours? If there was or is now such a person, it must be St. Padre Pio, who wanted to love God so much God gave him His wounds so they could suffer together.

---

[1]   Ruffin, p. 74.
[2]   Ibid, p. 137.
[3]   Ibid, p. 140.
[4]   Pio, 2018, p. 57.
[5]   Ibid, pp. 174–75.
[6]   da Cervinara, 1993, p. 47.
[7]   Pio, 2018, p. 175.
[8]   Ibid, p. 174.
[9]   Pope John Paul II. "Canonization of St. Pio of Pietrelcina."
[10] Wiersbe, p.189.

How to Become a Spiritual Child of Padre Pio

The spirituality of Padre Pio attracts those who hunger for heavenly knowledge, guidance from above and a meaningful way to live their faith. The words of Padre Pio reassure us of his love for us today and his continual guidance in our present lives.

> I belong entirely to everyone. Everyone can say: "Padre Pio is mine." I love my spiritual children as much as I love my own soul and even more. I have regenerated them to Jesus through suffering and love. I can forget myself, but not my spiritual children. Indeed, I can assure you, that when the Lord calls me, I will say to Him: "Lord, I will remain at the gates of Paradise; I will go in when I have seen the last of my children enter."[1]
>
> Rest assured I will pray for you. Even after my death I will remember you in my prayers… You must understand the responsibility I have assumed before Jesus for you. If something bad should happen to you which is to your spiritual detriment, Jesus will ask me to account for it directly…in me you will always have a father.[2]

To those who asked to be his spiritual children, he gave these conditions. We need only ask him, in faith, to be our spiritual father.

- Live immensely on God's grace and make use of the sacraments: the Eucharist and reconciliation.
- Live one's faith in words and actions in a true Christian life.
- Love Jesus Christ crucified, the Most Blessed Sacrament, our Blessed Mother, the Holy Father and the Roman Catholic Church.
- Be proactive and animated by a sincere spirit of charity toward all.

---

[1] Ruffin, p. 74.
[2] Allen, 2011, p. 145.

Padre Pio Prayer Groups

The Prayer Groups are a response to the spiritual needs
of our times as perceived by Padre Pio of Pietrelcina.
—Foreword of the New Statutes of the
Prayer Groups of Padre Pio

Preceding World War II, in an effort to organize his children and utilize the praying power they held, Padre Pio followed the call from Pope Pius XII to gather together his spiritual children from around the world to pray. He knew the praying power of the groups when he said, "Many, many more will come in the future, and my arms will stretch out until I can embrace the whole world."

The following is an outline determined by the International Association of Padre Pio Prayer Groups for establishing a prayer group at a parish.

* * * * *

When there are five people willing to commit to a prayer group, find a priest who is willing to direct your group. He will be called the Spiritual Director. He may, or may not, be a priest from your parish. The basic purpose of a Director is to keep the group true to Saint Pio's purpose of the prayer group and the teachings of the Catholic Church. Before the group can exist, it must receive a blessing from the head parish priest. Be ready to state the difference between the Padre Pio Prayer Group and other prayer groups.

Once a Director is found, registration forms necessary for the formation and establishment of the group must be completed. These can be found at the websites below. The group must choose officers from the group. The following are offices:

- Group Leader
- Vice-Group Leader
- Secretary
- Web Person (optional)
- Leader of Young People (optional)

Once the registration forms are completed, send them to the bishop of your diocese with a cover letter on parish letterhead explaining the purpose of the prayer group. The bishop of the diocese must give permission for the group to proceed. If you need assistance writing to your bishop, your Spiritual Director should have his address and what should be stated.

When permission is given, the forms must be sent to two places: the Centro Gruppi address in San Giovanni, Italy, and the national headquarters in Delaware (see addresses previously given), along with cover letters explaining the purpose and process. Make copies of all documents sent and received. When the letter of recognition from San Giovanni is received, forward a copy to the national headquarters. Thereafter, send monthly activity reports to San Giovanni.

Upon completion of the process, the association will send an extremely nice large certificate for your group suitable for framing. Activities and responsibilities of the group can be viewed at the sites below.

* * * * *

Contact Information for International Padre Pio Prayer Groups

Centro Internazionale Gruppi Di Preghiera Di Padre Pio

Viale Cappuccini 172
Casa Sollievo della Sofferenza
71013 San Giovanni Rotondo, Italy
Tel. +39 0882410486
Tel. +39 0882410252
Fax +39 0882452579
Email: centrogruppidipreghiera@operapadrepio.it
Website: www.operapadrepio.it/gruppidipreghiera
Facebook: www.facebook.com/gruppidipreghiera/
WhatsApp: +39 341115695

Padre Pio Prayer Groups USA

St. Francis of Assisi
1901 Prior Road
Wilmington, Delaware 19809
Tel: (302) 798-1454
www.pppg.org
pppgusa@gmail.com

* * * * *

Free downloads, prayer cards, and bookmarkers at friendsofpadrepio.com

Stay With Me, Lord

Stay with me, Lord, for it is necessary to have You present so that I do not forget You.

You know how easily I abandon You.

Stay with me, Lord, because I am weak and I need Your strength, that I may not fall so often.

Stay with me, Lord, for You are my life; and without You, I am without fervor.

Stay with me, Lord, for You are my light; and without You, I am in darkness.

Stay with me, Lord, to show me Your will.

Stay with me, Lord, so that I hear Your voice and follow you.

Stay with me, Lord, for I desire to love You very much and always be in Your company.

Stay with me, Lord, if You wish me to be faithful to You.

Stay with me, Lord, for as poor as my soul is, I want it to be a place of consolation for You, a nest of love.

Stay with me, Jesus, for it is getting late and the day is coming to a close and life passes; death, judgment, eternity approaches. It is necessary to renew my strength so that I will not stop along the way, and for that, I need You. It is getting late and death approaches. I fear the darkness, the temptations, the dryness, the cross, the sorrows. O how I need You, my Jesus, in this night of exile.

Stay with me tonight, Jesus, in life with all its dangers, I need You.

Let me recognize You as Your disciples did at the breaking of the bread, so that the Eucharistic Communion be the Light which disperses the darkness, the force which sustains me, the unique joy of my heart.

Stay with me, Lord, because at the hour of my death, I want to remain united to You, if not by Communion, at least by grace and love.

Stay with me, Jesus, I do not ask for divine consolation because I do not merit it, but the gift of Your presence, oh yes, I ask this of You.

Stay with me, Lord, for it is You alone I look for, Your Love, Your Grace, Your Will, Your Heart, Your Spirit, because I love You and ask no other reward but to love You more and more. With a firm love, I will love you with all my heart while on earth and continue to love You perfectly during all eternity. Amen.

Efficacious Prayer to the Sacred Heart of Jesus

(Recited everyday by Padre Pio for all those who asked his prayers)

Oh, my Jesus, You have said,
"Truly, I say to you, ask and it will be given, seek and
you will find, knock and the door will be opened."
Behold! I knock, I seek and I ask for the grace (your intention)

Our Father… Hail Mary… Glory Be

Sacred Heart of Jesus, I place all my trust in You.
Oh, my Jesus, You have said,
"Truly I say to you, ask anything of the Father
in My name and He will give it to you."
Behold! In Your name, I ask the Father
for the grace (your intention)

Our Father… Hail Mary… Glory Be

Sacred Heart of Jesus, I place all my trust in You.
Oh, my Jesus, You have said,
"Heaven and earth will pass away, but My
words will never pass away."

Encouraged by Your infallible words, I ask
for the grace (your intention)
Our Father... Hail Mary... Glory Be

Sacred Heart of Jesus, I place all my trust in You.

Oh, Sacred Heart of Jesus, for Whom it is impossible not to
have compassion on the afflicted, have mercy on us sinners and
grant us the grace of which we ask, through the Sorrowful and
Immaculate Heart of Mary, Your tender Mother and ours.
Amen.

Act of Consecration to Mary

(Prayed by Padre Pio First Saturday of the month)

O Mary, Virgin most powerful and Mother of
mercy, Queen of Heaven and refuge of sinners, we
consecrate ourselves to your Immaculate Heart.
We consecrate to you our very being and our whole
life; all that we have, all that we love, all that we are.
To you we give our bodies, our hearts and our souls; to
you we give our homes, our families, our country.
We desire that all that is in us and around us may belong
to you, and may share in the benefits of your motherly
benediction. And, that this act of consecration may be truly
efficacious and lasting, we renew this day at your feet the
promises of our Baptism and our first Holy Communion.
We pledge ourselves to profess courageously and at
all times the truths, of our Holy Faith, and to live as
Catholics who are duly submissive to all the directions of
the pope and the bishops in communion with him.
We pledge ourselves to keep the commandments of God and
His church, in particular to keep holy the Lord's Day. We
likewise pledge ourselves to make the consoling practices of
the Christian religion, and above all, Holy Communion, an
integral part of our lives, in so far as we shall be able to do so.
Finally, we promise you, O glorious Mother of God and loving
Mother of all, to devote ourselves wholeheartedly to your service,
in order to hasten and assure, through the sovereignty of your

Immaculate Heart, the coming of the kingdom of the Sacred Heart
of your adorable Son, in our own hearts and in the hearts of all,
in our country and in all the world, as in heaven, so on earth.
Amen.

Alberto, D. P. *Padre Pio of Pietrelcina. Memories. Experiences. Testimonials.* San Giovanni Rotondo: Edizioni Padre Pio, 2007.

Allen, D. *Pray, Hope, and Don't Worry: True stories of Padre Pio, Book 2.* San Diego, California: Padre Pio Press, 2011.

————. *Pray, Hope, and Don't worry: True stories of Padre Pio, Book 1.* San Diego, CA: Padre Pio Press, 2012.

Amorth, G., and S. Stimamiglio. *An Exorcist Explains the Demonic: The Antics of Satan and His Army of Fallen Angels* (C. J. Fasi, Trans.). Manchester, New Hampshire: Sophia Institute Press, 2016.

Avila, Saint Teresa of. *The Complete Works of St. Teresa: The Life of St. Teresa of Jesus.* [eBook edition]. Omaha, Nebraska: Patristic Publishing, 2019.

Benincasa, C. *The Dialogue of St. Catherine of Siena.* (A. Thorold, Trans.) Charlotte: TAN Books, 2010.

Capuano, P. *Con P. Pio: Come In Una Fiaba.* Foggia: Grafiche Grilli, 2012.

Castelli, F. *Padre Pio Under Investigation. The Secret Vatican Files.* San Francisco: Ignatius Press, 2011.

Catherine. *The Dialogue of St. Catherine of Siena: Dictated by Her, while in the State of Ecstasy, to her Secretaries, and Completed in the year of Our Lord 1370: Together with an Account of Her Death by an Eyewitness.* (A. Thorold, Trans.). Charlotte, NC: Saint Benedict Press, TAN Books, 2010.

"Catholic Life Ministries, Archive » 'I Thirst'—a Letter from Mother Teresa to Her Sisters." Scribbr. April 18, 2019. http://www.catholiclifeministries.org/2019/04

Chambers, O. *My Utmost for His Highest Journal.* Uhrichsville, Ohio: Barbour Pub, 1997.

Chiron, Y. *Padre Pio. Una Strada di Misericordia.* Milano: Figlie di San Paolo, 1999.

D'Apolito, A. *Padre Pio da Pietrelcina. Ricordi, Esperienze, Testimonianze.* San Giovanni Rotondo: Edizioni Padre Pio, 2010.

da Cervinara, Tarcisco. *Padre Pio's Mass.* San Giovanni Rotondo: La Casa Sollievo della Sofferenza, 1983.

da Riese, F. *Padre Pio da Pietrelcina Crocifisso Senza Croce.* San Giovanni Rotondo: Edizioni Padre Pio, 2010.

De Liso, O. *Padre Pio.* New York: All Saints Press, 1962.

Duchess Suzanne, O. S. *Magic of a Mystic. Stories of Padre Pio.* New York: Clarkson N. Potter, 1983.

Epistolario I. *Corrispondenza con i Direttori Spirituali (1910–1922).* San Giovanni Rotondo: Edizioni Padre Pio, 2011.

Epistolario III. *Corrispondenza con le Figlie Spirituali (1915–1923).* San Giovanni Rotondo: Edizioni Padre Pio, 2012.

Epistolario IV. *Corrispondenza con Diverse Categorie di Persone.* San Giovanni Rotondo: Edizioni Padre Pio, 2012.

Frankl, V. *Man's search for meaning.* New York: Pocket Books, 1976.

Galeone, Dom P. *Padre Pio Mio Padre.* Cinisello Balsamo: Edizioni San Paolo, 2009.

———. "Together With Padre Pio: Booklet One." September 18, 2015. *www.lecatechesididonvincenzocarone.wordpress.com.* INSIEME CON PADRE PIO—Booklet I.

Gautrelet, Fr. François-Xavier. *Morning Offering Prayer: Catholic Household Blessings and Prayers.* Washington DC: United States Conference of Catholic Bishops, 1989.

Iasenzaniro, F. M. *The "Padre" Saint Pio of Pietrelcina. His Mission to Save Souls. Testimonies.* San Giovanni Rotondo: Edizioni Padre Pio, 2006.

Iasenzaniro, M. *Charismatic Priest. Testimonies.* San Giovanni Rotondo: Edizioni Padre Pio, 2007.

Ingoldsby, M. *Padre Pio. His Life and Mission.* Dublin: Veritas Publications, 1978.

Jezus, T. O. and J. Clarke. *Story of a soul: The Autobiography of Saint Thérèse of Lisieux.* Washington DC: ICS Publications, 1996.

Kempis, Thomas. *Imitation of Christ.* (ED: Richard Challoner). Charlotte: Saint Benedict/TAN Books, 2011.

Kowalska, M. F. *Diary of Saint Maria Faustina Kowalska: Divine Mercy in My Soul.* Stockbridge, Massachusetts: Marian Press, 2014.

Lewis, C. S. *The Worlds Last Night, and Other Essays.* San Francisco: HarperOne, 2017.

Lisieux, T. *Story of a soul: The autobiography of Saint Thérèse of Lisieux.* (J. Clarke, Trans.). Washington D. C.: ICS Publications, 1996.

Marison, F. (Trans.). *City of God: Popular Abridgement of the Divine History and Life of the Virgin Mother of God.* Charlotte, North Carolina: Tan Books, 1978.

McGlynn, T. M. *Vision of Fatima.* Manchester, New Hampshire: Sophia Institute Press, 2017.

Michalenko, S. *The Life of Faustina Kowalska: The Authorized Biography.* Cincinnati, Ohio: Servant Books, 1999.

Morcaldi, C. *La Mia Vita Vicino a Padre Pio.* San Giovanni Rotondo: Edizioni Casa Sollievo della Sofferenza. Quinta Edizione, 2013.

Napolitano, F. *Padre Pio of Pietrelcina. A Brief Biography.* San Giovanni Rotondo: Edizioni Padre Pio, 1979.

Parente, A. *Padre Pio e Le Anime del Purgatorio.* San Giovanni Rotondo: Edizioni Padre Pio, 2011.

Parente, Alessio. *The Holy Souls.* San Giovanni Rotondo: Edizioni PadrePio, 2015.

Pasquale, G., O.F.M. Cap. (Ed.). *Secrets of a Soul: Padre Pio's Letters to His Spiritual Director.* (E. G. Di Fabio Ph.D., Trans.). Boston, Massachusetts: Pauline Books & Media, 2003.

Pearson, S. E. *Faithful Celebrations: Making Time for God with the Saints.* New York: Church Publishing, 2019.

Peroni, L. *Padre Pio da Pietrelcina.* Borla, 2012.

Pio. *Padre Pio's Words of Hope.* (E. D. Bertanzetti, Ed.). Huntington, Indiana: Our Sunday Visitor Pub. Division, Our Sunday Visitor, 1999.

Pio. *Secrets of a Soul: Padre Pio's Letters to His Spiritual Director.* (G. Pasquale, Ed.; E. G. DiFabio, Trans.). Boston, Massachusetts: Pauline Books & Media, 2003.

Pio. *Have A Good Day.* (Ed. Mariano di Vito). San Giovanni Rotondo: Edizioni Padre Pio, 2010.

Pio. *Have a Good Day.* (Bro. F. Scaramuzzi, Ed.) San Giovanni Rotondo: Edizioni Padre Pio, 2018.

Pio. I Am Consumed by Love for God. *The Voice of Padre Pio* 4. 2021.

Pope John Paul II. "Apostolic Letter Salvifici Doloris of the Supreme Pontiff John Paul II to the Bishops, to the Priests, to the Religious Families and to the Faithful of the Catholic Church on the Christian Meaning of Human Suffering." February 11, 1984. http://www.vatican.va/content/john-paul-ii/en/apost_letters/1984/ documents/hf_jp-ii_apl_11021984_salvifici-do-loris.html. Libreria Editrice Vaticana.

Ratzinger, Joseph. "Das Fest des Glaubens. Versuche zur Theologie des Gottesdienstes" (Feast of Faith: Approaches to a Theology of the Liturgy). Johannes, Einsiedeln, 1993 (III ed.), pp. 84–85 (J. Ratzinger, Theologie der Liturgie. Die sakramentale Begründung christlicher Existenz, Gesammelte Schriften 11, Friburgo, Herder 2008, p. 626).

Ruotolo, Sac. Dolindo. *Che Significa Dolore—Fui Chiamato Dolindo, Che Significa Dolore... Paigine D'Autobiografia.* Naples: Dell'Apostolato Stampa, 1972.

Ruffin, C. B. *Padre Pio: The True Story.* Huntington, IN: Our Sunday Visitor Publishing Division, Our Sunday Visitor, 2018.

Schug, J. O. *A Padre Pio Profile.* Petersham: St. Bedès Publications, 1987.

Tangari, K. *Stories of Padre Pio* (J. Collorati, Trans.). Rockville, Illinois: Tan Bks, 1996.

Teresa. *Mother Teresa: Come Be My Light; The Private Writings of the Saint of Calcutta* (B. Kolodiejchuk, Ed.). New York: Image, 2007.

Thigpen, Paul. *Manual for Spiritual Warfare.* Charlotte, Charlotte: TAN Books, 2014.

Vanauken, Sheldon. *A Severe Mercy.* New York: HarperCollins, 1997.

Vianney, J. *The Little Catechism of the Cure of Ars.* Rockford, Illinois: Tan Books, 2011.

Wiersbe, W. W. *50 People Every Christian Should Know: Learning from Spiritual Giants of the Faith.* Grand Rapids, Michigan: Baker Books, 2009.

Winowska, M. *Il Vero Volto di Padre Pio.* Milano: Edizioni San Paolo, 1988.

Additional Resources for Prayers

St. Teresa of Avila (1515–1582) offered a method for the meditative or interior form of prayer, which Peter Thomas Rohrbach sums well in his book *Conversation with Christ*. The outline of meditation is as follows:

1. *Prepare to meet God*—find a quiet spot. Clear your mind. Find yourself in Him by acknowledging His presence. Say three times, "Come, Holy Spirit."
2. *Select material to meditate*—read from scripture, a devotional, or the biography of a saint. Choose a specific prayer (Rosary, novena, chaplet). Bring to mind your personal joys, concerns, or prayer requests. These are what you will speak to God about.
3. *Meditate*—reflect on the material you chose. What is the idea behind the material? What is it saying to me? What does this have to do with me? How does this reflect who I am or need to be? Own your thoughts and feelings.
4. *Talk with God*—speak your thankfulness, fears, or questions. Ask, "What are You asking of me? What in me is not of You?" Share your thoughts and feelings, joys and hurts. In your mind's eye, see Him looking at you, laughing with you, crying with you, holding you. If there is a specific concern, pray, "Lord, I surrender myself to You. You take care of it." Be silent if needed.
5. *Conclusion*—pray these words: "Lord, I give You what You take from me, and I receive what You give me. Take

from me what You need to help those I pray for. Make me the person You wish of me. I give myself to You." Pray for others. At this time, you may ask for the intercession of Mother Mary or any saint.

These steps require effort. So set aside a place and time to meet Him. Be ready to open yourself to all that He is. When I pray, Jesus tells me, "Embrace Me on My Cross, and I will embrace you on yours."

*****

St. Ignatius of Loyola (1491–1556) created a system of spiritual exercises that would help reform a person into the image of their Creator. This form of prayer is called the Examen. These exercises would be practiced in a retreat or adapted for personal prayer. The three basic exercises are interior.

1. *Examen*—reflect on the condition of the soul—its strengths, weaknesses, desires, and loves. Reflect when during the day these conditions appear. Present them to God for His removal or strengthening of them. Choose one as an offering to strengthen or diminish as He determines. Pray, "LORD, remove all that is not of You." Determine a prayer of gratitude or repentance when they occur such an Our Father or Hail Mary. This may be done at the start of the day. At the day's end, reflect on how it turned out. After reflection, seek His guidance on how to approach them the next day. Search Him out in the details, then surrender yourself to His will in these matters.

2. *Meditation*—when examining the day, use the *memory* to bring the day's occurrences to mind, to see what you committed to God happening. When the condition of the soul showed itself, which won out, grace or sin? This is the *understanding* of the matter. In the end, all that is not of God must go.

3. *Contemplation*—we apply our *senses* to the matter. We "see" ourselves with Jesus helping us accomplish what we have placed in His Hands and experience His Spirit working in us. (If the *Examen* identifies sin in our life to destroy it, *Contemplation* helps to experience His love and presence in our life to overcome it.)

Slowly, methodically, in and with and through faith, this method of prayer—if consistent and done with complete surrender—takes all that is not of God out of our lives. It is self-purification. It is our sanctification.

Helpful Catholic apps to guide prayer include Hallow, Laudate, and Reimagining the Examen, an online version of the Examen.

About the Author

M. L. Moncayo is a retired educator living in Southern California with his wife and family. A spiritual child of Padre Pio, he wrote *The Way of Padre Pio* from the monthly newsletter he wrote for the Padre Pio Prayer Group at his parish. Reading volumes of literature on St. Pio, he realized there was no material written specifically on the spiritual principles Padre Pio lived by. He sought a simple way to explain in everyday words and examples the principles of Redemptive Suffering in the saint's own words so they may live out the principles in their everyday lives.

9 798888 751107 8